Cover design by Design One Media Group
www.d1mg.com

DEDICATION

To Ross, thank you for being secure enough to let me start exploring this project!!

To Dave, thank you for being the guinea pig in this project!! You are appreciated more than you know!

To Carrie, thank you for being willing to use "some" red ink to help get this project to this point!

To Whitneyville Bible Church, what an amazing thing we have seen God do in our church!

To Caleb, Andrew, and Rebecca, thank you for letting your dad work so many late Monday nights to get this entire project completed!! I love you guys so much!!

Finally, to Kimberly, thank you for your support, encouragement, patience, and willingness to let me go through this entire process!! I couldn't have done it without you!! I love you!

Forward

Let me commend to you the written "journey" you hold in your hands. You can trust the leader of this ecclesiastical hike as he personally takes us on an important jaunt over the too often toxic landscape of church leadership. The core of this work looks specifically at how a congregation protects itself when considering what kind of elders should lead them. The reader is faced with a variety of considerations the typical congregation should be aware of in regard to a right process of bringing the right kind of spiritual leaders to the positions that are needed for church-health. Once you have identified a potential leader, a great follow-up question is, "should there be any consideration for training and preparation for the office of elder" or do we simply throw the new guy out into the deep side of the pool? So if there is a process, what does that look like? Dave asks these questions in large part because he's tired of seeing the ongoing destructive effects of bad leadership in organizational ministry.

Dave Deets is no stranger to this journey. Like most guides he has the needed equipment to get us from one side of the canyon to the other. He knows where the trail becomes especially volatile and hazardous both for the individual and for the ministry. He's been on the bruising side of walking the canyon before without the necessary equipment in previous chapters of life and ministry. The knowledge he's picked up along the way has highly motivated him to be there for others. As his good friend I can tell you Dave is particularly interested in helping both elders and the ministries they lead to have a biblical, vocational and practical clarity on a variety of issues that will haunt the careless ministry that has a track record of simply rushing through a process so as to fill some kind of a "leadership quota." Dave ends the book by giving a helpful slate of suggestion when facing special and unique challenges with the process of bringing elders (and even other key leaders) into positions of leadership especially when the congregation is blinded to the realities of their mired sub-culture.

It is my sincere pleasure to introduce this work by way of written forward. Dave has become one of my dearest brothers and closest friends in the Lord's army of Christian workers. Dave has begun to serve with me and the rest of our IBL colleagues as he helps us in "side by side" ministry to leaders here in North America and around the planet at the Institute of Biblical Leadership (www.iblministry.org). It is therefore with a heart full of thanksgiving and enthusiasm I commend this work to you. As you take these principles and utilize them in your own ministries my prayer is that God will grant you strength as you faithfully plow in your corner of our Lord's Vineyard.

Straight Ahead!

Dr. Joel Tetreau,
Lead Pastor, *Southeast Valley Bible Church* (Gilbert, AZ)
Western Regional Coordinator, *Institute of Biblical Leadership*
Author, "*The Pyramid and the Box: The Decision-Making Process in a local New Testament Church*" (Wipf and Stock Publishers, 2013)

Contents

Introduction

It is a rainy Sunday morning in Nairobi, Kenya. The streets are muddy as running water washes down the side of the road. This morning, a young Pastor and his family will make their way to church where about one hundred other believers will gather to worship. These believers are from all over Africa. Refugees from the Congo and South Sudan and Tanzania will worship together with men and women from Nairobi and the outlying areas. All of them have found a place of refuge in Nairobi. Many of them are uneducated and have little Biblical training.

Pastor Fred is charged with the task of teaching and training these future leaders with the truths of God's word. His commission is the same as any other pastor; equip the saints to do the work of the ministry. Now, as he oversees three different churches, Pastor Fred must find a way to ensure that he has qualified men in place to be elders of the churches that are being established. This scenario repeats itself all over Nairobi in various churches across this great city. How will the pastors of these churches find men who are qualified to be elders?

In Orleans, France, a missionary meets with about forty people in a hotel lobby for Sunday worship. Men and women from various backgrounds and various occupations gather in this small group to worship together each Sunday. How will this missionary find the right men to serve as elders in the church? How will he ensure that he has effectively reproduced himself in the lives of these people? Again, this scenario repeats itself all over Europe as other missionaries and pastors seek to be faithful to the call of God in their life.

It is 5:00am in Vietnam and a middle-aged man rushes to meet other men from his church for a Bible study. It is still dark as he makes his way, by bicycle, to the meeting place. He has learned to be careful in how he moves about the city, so as not to draw attention to himself. In this Southeast Asian country, the gospel is not openly received. He has been meeting for several weeks with the pastor of his church along with other faithful men from the church to be taught and trained in the work of an elder. Being a church leader is a risky position for this man, but one he believes God desires him to have. What qualities and attributes should this man possess in order to be an elder in the church in Southeast Asia?

It is Sunday afternoon in Southern California. Pastor Jim has just finished preaching the Sunday morning service at his church. The four thousand people that gathered this morning at Faith Community Church have been encouraged to be proactive in the Christian walk and to allow God to use them as He sees fit. Now as he sits in his chair in his living room he wonders how he can continue to encourage the men of His church to step up into leadership and join him as elders to serve and to shepherd the flock of God there in Southern California. Does he have the right men in leadership, and how should he pursue bringing other men on as elders?

The needs of Pastor Jim are the same as the needs of Pastor Fred and the same as the needs of the Pastors in Southeast Asia, and the same as the needs of the missionary in Europe. What does it take to be an elder? Who should lead the church? How do we know who is qualified? Does it really matter how we select our elders? Is there a right way or wrong way to go about bringing men into leadership in church? All of these questions are necessary and thought provoking at the same time. Every pastor has had to wrestle through these challenging scenarios, and every pastor will be accountable for how he leads the congregation of the local church God has sent him to shepherd.

Some Clarity... Defining the Words....

As with all conversations, it is important that we are all on the same page as to what is being discussed and how words and thoughts are being defined. This topic is no different. In order to ensure that we are clear on terms, I will seek to define a few of the terms that will be used in this book.

Elder – A man who fulfills the biblical requirements of I Timothy 3 and Titus 1. He has a calling of God on his life to serve the church as a pastor and is willing to serve, paid or unpaid, in the church. He is tasked with the role of oversight of the congregation, he is to provide shepherding and pastoral care for the congregation, he is to be able to adequately teach and defend the word of God. This man is distinct from a deacon—a man called by God to serve the congregation in ministering to the physical needs of the church. The elder is not a deacon, and the deacon is not an elder. These are two distinct positions filled by two distinct people.

Plurality – Having more than one biblically qualified man who serves as elder of a local church. This is in contrast to a church who would see a "single-headed" leadership of a head pastor.

Equality – Having equal authority in both position and in decision-making ability. There is not one man who has more power or authority than the other men who serve as elders. There may be a lead elder or an elder who is seen as the "face" of the church, but he has no more authority than the other elders. All elders are equal in authority.

Polity – The organizational structure of the leadership of a local church. How they view the authority structure of their leaders and how they view the role of the congregation is considered their polity. It is their way of governing the church.

My Story...Briefly...

I grew up in and served as an assistant pastor in Baptist churches where the term elder would not have been used. In fact the concept of elders would have been somewhat of a foreign idea to the churches. During my time as an associate pastor at a church in Denver, I began to be intrigued by the idea of elders and eldership and began to study, research, and discuss biblical eldership. It was during this time that God opened the door for me to develop a friendship with Alex Strauch, author of, *Biblical Eldership.*

I was being challenged from several different vantage points to dive into Scripture to know with confidence what the Bible had to say about church leadership, specifically elders. I knew that what I had experienced growing up may not have been easily defended in Scripture, but the hold and the default which my upbringing held on me was very strong. I knew that I needed to study and be willing to change if necessary, but I also knew what I had been taught for most of my church life. As it turns out, God was graciously leading me where He wanted me to go. I just needed to follow.

As God would see fit, I had the opportunity to become the lead pastor of a Bible Church near Grand Rapids, Michigan. As I arrived, I was informed that the current elders of the church had decided that the new pastor would be responsible for establishing a process for selecting elders. This had come about as a result of some strong tension that had existed in the church for years regarding how the church historically had chosen elders. For me, stepping into my first lead pastorate was difficult and scary enough. To become the pastor of a church that had elders was even more challenging, as this was an entirely new polity model for me. To arrive and be told, we would like you to help us figure out how to select elders, all the while getting used to being a lead pastor and getting used to a new polity, was more of a daunting task than I wanted to think about.

8

Needless to say, I was a bit overwhelmed. Not knowing anything else to do, I decided that we would look only to Scripture to identify the various components for elders mentioned in Scripture and then we would establish the criteria that needed to be met in order for a man to be considered as an elder. I knew that I personally did not have the answers for the church, but I did have confidence in the Word of God and its sufficiency for the needs that our church was facing.

Shortly after I arrived, I met with the four current men who filled the office of elder at the time, and I began to ask them what they had to do to become elders at the church. In my mind, the best thing I could do was to start with some sort of baseline of what we were dealing with to see where we needed to go. Some of the men were elders because other people had told them that they should be an elder. Some had become an elder for the sake of church stability, even though they personally did not have a desire to be an elder. Some liked the idea of being an elder, but felt inadequate in certain elements of functionality as an elder.

One of the things that was clear in talking with these men was, as they admitted, that they really did not have a good idea or system in place for selecting elders. In fact, one response that was given was that they did not know how to select elders. I told the men that they did in fact know how to select elders, since they had just selected me. There was certainly some mental processing going on as they evaluated what was being said. In fact, one responded, very understandably, "You really want us to go through what we put you through?" It was clear that there was work to be done, however, I wasn't exactly aware of just how much work it would take. There was a lot I did not know then and still don't know today, but I knew that If they wanted to have equality among the elders, they would have to go through a similar process to what they put me through in choosing me as the lead pastor. That would be the only way to ensure that we had biblically qualified men who desired to be elders actually serving as elders.

What transpired over the next several months became the impetus for my doctoral dissertation, and eventually the idea for this book. It was a bit of a journey to not only identify the various elements that needed to be accounted for in the lives of the elders, but also to have the men and ultimately the congregation trust God's word enough to implement this process. This has been a challenging process for our church, but it has been a rewarding process as well. God has blessed and has brought a spirit of unity in this process to the congregation. It has been a thrill to see what happens when we trust the sufficiency of God and His word.

The Purpose of This Book...

The purpose of this book is to lay out the Biblical basis for why and how the right men must be selected for leadership in the church. Some of you are no doubt part of a church that has an incredible handle on the elder selection process. To that end, I hope that this book is an encouragement to you and you can use this as a resource in your ministry. However, I understand that many others reading this do not have a working process for selecting elders. Maybe this is because you have never given it much thought, or maybe it is because it seemed to be too daunting of a task to try to get something together. Whatever the reason, I am thrilled that you are reading this, and I pray that it will be a blessing and encouragement to you and your ministry.

This book is designed to be read by any believer who has an interest in the topic of eldership of a church. Specifically, it is written for someone who has an interest in how to select elders in a church. This book is designed to work whether it is in the context of a non-denominational church, a Baptist church, a Presbyterian church or any other church where elders are used

10

in the polity of the church. It is also designed to be able to be used in any context around the world. It is geared to work with the Bakka people in Cameroon, the Navajo people of New Mexico, and everywhere elders are used. The reason for the global and diverse usability of this book is that it is based upon the truths of God's word.

This book is not meant to be the only book used on the topic of elder selection. However, it is designed and intended to be a practical, hands-on guide to the selection of elders. There are multiple variations that can be employed in selecting elders. This book can be a great resource for you and your ministry as you strive to select the right men for church leadership.

I pray that this book will be a blessing and encouragement to you and to all those who read it for the glory of God!

1

Welcome to First Church of Good Intentions

What happens when you don't
have a biblical selection process?

Meet Sam. Sam is a 47-year-old plumber. He works hard each day providing for his family and he is engaged at his church. On this particular night, Sam is heading to the church for an elder's meeting. Sam doesn't really want to go to the meeting, not because he won't enjoy seeing the other men, but primarily because he has no real love, desire, or passion for being an elder. He is glad that by being on the elder team, he has the opportunity to make decisions and take action on behalf of the church, but Sam does not see himself as a pastor and he certainly does not want to be involved in shepherding the believers of his church. Sam feels that his job as an elder is to show up to meetings and make decisions. Sam loves God and he loves serving, but Sam has no real desire to serve as an elder.

Meet Rick. Rick is a 67-year-old retiree. He has some free time since he is retired and when someone nominated Rick to be an elder at his church, he thought "Sure, I could probably do that." Rick isn't too sure about what he believes theologically, but he does not perceive that to be a deal breaker in being an elder. The church Rick attends does not see the importance of asking any theological or doctrinal questions of their prospective elders, so Rick believes he is "good to go" as an elder. After all, he sees his primary role as keeping an eye on the pastor and making some spiritual decisions every now and then. Rick knows that he has some questions about God and some positions doctrinally that aren't necessarily held by others in the church, but he figures since no one asked him about them, he didn't need to share his thoughts on the matter.

Meet Greg. Greg is a "rough around the edges" 36-year-old construction worker. He won't hesitate to tell you what he thinks and he can be a bit abrasive. Some people in the church like him because of that; some don't like him because of that. However, as a construction worker, Greg has a bad reputation among the unsaved guys that he works with. He is known to regularly lose his temper, cuss "with the best of them", and show little if any respect for his bosses. But, since no one at church felt it was necessary to check his reputation with those who are outside the church, Greg serves as an elder, no one thinks anything about what his life and testimony are like outside of the church.

Meet Mike. Mike is 56 and is a quiet, somewhat reserved accountant at a local accounting firm. He serves as an elder only because he wants to help the church have some stability. After-all, this really fits his personality type of not liking change and chaos. He likes things to remain fairly constant and unchanged, and he sees his role as maintaining quiet continuity in the church. His accountant background really encourages this. He feels he plays a valuable role in the life of the church by making sure that the church is run like a well-oiled machine and that it does not do anything too drastic or too quick. Mike loves the Lord, but really is not into the whole "elder thing," and he is simply biding his time until his term ends.

Is there anything wrong with having Sam, Rick, Greg, or Mike as elders of your church? What if these are the best guys you can find? Is it okay that these men are serving as elders? What does Scripture say about the qualification of these men? Are you okay as the lead elder with these men serving the church as elders? If so, why? If not, why not?

13

It seems safe to assume that the vast majority of biblically engaged, evangelical churches have a desire to follow God's word. The issue is not so much the desire, but rather it is the know how that some churches struggle with. How do we implement what God has told us to do in His word? Is it worth the fight and the hassle? Does it really matter anyway? Some churches get so frustrated with the challenges of engaging in the completion of God's word that they simply allow pragmatism to set in and seek anything that works. Others try hard, but just simply never seem to figure things out in the practical life of the church.

Many churches could have the name, First Church of Good Intentions. They have the best thoughts in mind, but when it comes to the actual implementation of these biblical principles they just come up short. They mean really well and they want to do what God desires, but the know how or the resolve to do what God intends is not there.

Is it really a big deal though? God is gracious and merciful. God is loving and caring. God is long-suffering and understanding. Does it really matter if we don't select the right men to be elders? Can't we just be okay with good guys who have good hearts? Isn't it good enough to ask these guys if they agree to our statement of faith? Can't we just assume that since they love Jesus that they will make good elders? Do we really need a process for selecting the right men to be elders?

The answer to these questions is that it does matter who you have as elders in your church. The Bible is extremely clear on the necessary elements in this process of selecting the right men to be elders. The Bible is also clear that as a pastor and as a church you must have the integrity to follow the biblical pattern for finding biblically qualified men to serve as elders. Failure to select biblically qualified men will result in debilitating consequences that will eventually embed themselves in the DNA of the church.

The following challenges are certainly not comprehensive, nor are they all present in every church that does not have a biblical process for selecting elders. However, some of these, and potentially all of these, will be present to one degree or another in the church that fails to follow the biblical process for selecting their elders. Each of these are deadly to the overall health of the church and will, if not dealt with, cause severe harm to the body.

Scriptural Incompleteness

The point of Scripture, namely I Timothy 3 and Titus 1, telling us all about the elder, is that these markers of Scripture were intended to be implemented in an elder selection process. When it comes to some churches, the prospective elders are asked if they are willing to serve, but they are never asked to describe their calling. When Paul said that if a man aspires to the office of bishop, (I Timothy 3:1 The saying is trustworthy: If anyone aspires to the office of overseer, he desires a noble task), the Greek word he used was the word for reaching out or snatching something. This means that a man who is planning to be an elder, should have an active engagement in the process. He should be communicating his call/desire to serve as an elder based upon the work that God is doing in his heart. The prospective elders at some churches are only being asked if they are willing to fulfill a temporary role of administrative oversight. That, in some cases, means they function as glorified deacons.

When a church does not ask a man to describe his call, to describe his desire to reach out and grab the office of elder, then their process is scripturally incomplete. Every prospective elder needs to be able to effectively communicate his desire to be an elder. Failure to do that results in the process being scripturally incomplete

Doctrinal Deficiency

Some churches take the opinion that if a man just simply agrees to the church's statement of faith, then that is all the testing and checking they need to do on the man's doctrinal positions. The thought process is that since he agreed to the doctrinal statement, he must believe it and accept it. However, Titus 1 speaks definitively of the need for elders to be able to not only know God's word, but to be able to defend it. This is seen in Titus 1:9 where Paul tells Titus to make sure that they can hold firm to the word of God in order that they will not only be able to teach the Word, but also that they would be able to rebuke those who contradict God's word. "He must hold firm to the trustworthy word as taught, so that he may be able to give instruction in sound doctrine and also to rebuke those who contradict it". Simply agreeing to the doctrinal statement of the church does not adequately qualify a man for the fulfillment of Titus 1:9.

The Bible also speaks clearly (I Peter 5:2 shepherd the flock of God that is among you, exercising oversight) about the need for the elders to provide oversight for the body. This means, in part, that the elders are to be looking out over society at things happening in culture. As well, they should be looking over the church, to help warn and prepare the church for the various matters that the church will face. If there is not a doctrinal examination of the prospective elders, then how can the church be assured that these men, whom they have chosen as elders, are actually capable of defending the church against the false teachers? Affirming a statement of faith is entirely different than confidently defending the church against false doctrine. Affirmation says, "I agree to that" while defending it says, "I know and understand that and I can articulate why what a false teacher is saying is wrong."

Ecclesiastical Anemia

Another danger that can occur within the church when they do not have a biblical model of selecting elders is that of anemia. Anemia is a medical condition, which occurs when the blood does not have enough healthy red blood cells. The result of anemia is fatigue and becoming lethargic. In the world of a church, ecclesiastical anemia results in apathy or indifference among the body of Christ.

When the wrong men are in leadership and they begin to make decisions that are not in line with what Christ would desire for his church, that church will most likely experience anemia, leading to an apathetic and indifferent spirit. At times they fail to properly lead the church as they should and in some cases, they foster an environment of a good ol' boys club mindset of the eldership. When this occurs, the church begins to develop a political environment, which makes it incredibly difficult for the believers to function as they are supposed to function.

When ecclesiastical anemia occurs, the church will become extremely ineffective for the cause of Christ and a spirit of apathy will set in. This will result in carelessness about the things of God and His word, and it will result in the church as a whole not having a zeal or desire for worship, evangelism, discipleship, service, or anything that Christ would want His bride to be passionate about.

Ambiguous Functionality of the Role of Elder

An additional danger of not having a biblical model of selecting elders is that if the process is not biblical, then there is a really strong chance that there is not sufficient biblical training on the role of elders. In many cases, there is not a functional concept of the role of shepherding, oversight, or general pastoral care. The elders, in some cases, can seem to be disengaged from their obligation to shepherd the people. There is a sense that the

17

lead pastor's job is to shepherd, do hospital calls, and provide general care for the people. If they have to, the other elders could get involved in some matters of shepherding, but for the most part the job of shepherding falls to the lead pastor. In many cases, the concept of shepherding, on the part of the lay elders, is never enforced let alone communicated as part of their job.

Peter is clear in I Peter 5:1-5 that as fellow elders (sympresbuteros – elders together) all elders are to shepherd the flock of God among them. This means that all elders are to be engaged in the four major responsibilities of shepherding.

1. All elders are to care for the flock (James 5:14).
2. All elders are to oversee the flock (Titus 1:7).
3. All elders are to protect the flock through doctrinal integrity (Titus 1:9).
4. All elders are to equip the flock (Ephesians 4:11-12)

In some cases, the elders see themselves as the administrative oversight, a board of directors, that meet once a month (or more if absolutely needed) to review the services, make sure the Sunday School teachers have what they need and to make sure that things are functioning in the church. In reality, these men are not elders per se, (even though they have the title) as much as they are a board of directors or glorified deacons. They are given the elder title without the process being in place to become an elder. They see their role as governors who make sure the lead pastor stays in line with their wishes, instead of seeing themselves as teammates or fellow laborers for the cause of Christ. The lack of training and teaching on the role and the functionality of elders definitely hurts the relationship between the congregation and the leadership of the church.

Many times in this situation, the congregation is aware of the fact that the elders do not shepherd, and the congregation in turn bears the brunt of that misapplication--they are left to be shepherded by the lead elder by himself. The command of I

Peter 5 to shepherd the flock of God is seen by the lay elders to be the job of the senior pastor and not a job or function that they necessarily need to fill. This condition of the church makes everyone's roles fuzzy, and it becomes uncertain as to who is actually in charge and who is leading. Ambiguity on the part of the elders as to what they are to be doing is detrimental to the sheep that they are to be shepherding.

Inhibited Vision

One of the functional roles of the elder is to provide vision for the church. When men who are not called to be elders serve as elders, there can be little if any vision. This lack of vision plays itself out in many ways. For instance, there is no vision for how to raise up future elders. There is certainly a desire to have other men step up to become elders, but there is no practical vision of how to accomplish this.

In some cases, because there is no one to take their place, some elders will resort to guilt and/or manipulation to get others to serve as elders. The pattern of pushing or even guilting men into serving in the role of elder, not only violates I Timothy 3:1, but it is also extremely detrimental to that man's spiritual walk.

Because the men serving as elders struggle with vision for the church, this expresses itself in other areas as well. When there is no vision for future growth in the church or when there is no vision for spiritual maturity and discipleship for the congregation, the church will suffer. Whatever the challenge may be, Scripture is clear that vision and the life of the church are intrinsically linked. A church that does not have men serving as elders, who are actually qualified biblical elders, will be a church that is not healthy and a church that is not equipped for long-term biblical health. [Proverbs 28:19 Where there is no prophetic vision the people cast off restraint, but blessed is he who keeps the law]

Frustrated Burnout

Many churches struggle to not only have elders, but to keep elders continuously serving in the church. One of the real challenges that occurs when a church has men in place as elders who actually are not called by God to serve in that capacity is burnout. This is not to say that those men who are called by God and have a desire to be an elder never get burned out or never get frustrated with their role as an elder. However, the likelihood of a qualified man who is desirous to serve as an elder because that is God's calling in his life becoming burned out is actually pretty rare. He may need a break every now and then, but if he is called to be an elder, then that is a desire he should carry with him for life. Again, this does not mean that he never gets frustrated or always serves as an elder, but qualified men will have the leading of the Spirit guiding them and sustaining them through the challenges of eldership.

The sad reality is that a large number of men who serve as elders without being qualified or having a biblical desire to serve, will wind up stepping down as an elder as soon as their term is up, if not before. Some of this is due to the intense nature of the job of being an elder. Some is due to the pressures that the men face as they attempt to navigate the church through the difficult challenges that regularly confront a group of elders. Certainly these factors weigh heavy on the church as they struggle to survive these difficult challenges. There are several studies which indicate that between 1500 and 1700 pastors leave the ministry each month. Being called and qualified as an elder does not prevent this from happening, but it certainly helps.

A Blight in the Community

One of the devastating things that can take place when a church does not have a biblical model of selecting elders is the detrimental effects on the community. Whenever there is not biblically qualified men in place then the church will not function biblically as it is supposed to. When the church does not function properly, the consequences of the unbiblical leadership pours over into the community. When that happens, devastating results can become evident.

Take Mike for example. He has recently become the pastor of a small church in a rural Kansas town. As he begins to spend time in the community, he begins to hear comments such as, "Oh you are the new pastor at *that* church." After awhile the comments move from that to comments that are more damaging. For instance, consider the couple that worked for a Christian organization who, after moving to the area, were told that under no circumstances should they attend or even visit Mike's church because of the history and all of the issues that the church had witnessed. Consider as well, the situation at the office of a local doctor. Upon seeing Mike and realizing that he was the pastor of the church, the doctor proceeded to inform Mike of the leadership issues that had plagued the church for years. This man, a Catholic, had never attended the church, but after treating a number of patients for several decades had become intimately aware, with amazing accuracy and assessment, of the challenges and issues that the church had endured.

The challenge with having leadership that is not qualified biblically is the damaging effect that it has on the church itself. Sometimes it can be contained within the church and the testimony of Christ is not marred in the community. However, too often, the problems of the church overflow into the community and the name of Christ is damaged as is the reputation of the church. It is imperative for the cause of the gospel of Jesus Christ and His fame and reputation that the church be biblical in how it selects its leadership.

All of these are legitimate challenges that a church can face if they do not have the right men serving as elders in their church. The question then becomes how do we determine who should and who should not be an elder? What are the elements that must be present in a man's life in order to be considered as an elder? In the following chapters, we will attempt to lay out, as simply as possible, the biblical elements that must be accounted for in order to have qualified men serving as elders.

Again, we do not claim to have all of the answers, nor are we saying that everything in your process has to look exactly like our process. But if we can be a blessing to you and to your church and more importantly to the body of Christ as a whole, then we will be thrilled to help in any way we can. Please be diligent to search out what is said in this book to be sure it aligns with Scripture. To the point that it does align with Scripture, rejoice and use what you can from it. To the point that it does not align with Scripture, then ensure that you do not follow what is written in this book.

2

Let's Start at the Very Beginning

The Prospective Elder's Personal Evaluation

C.H. Spurgeon stated that to "Compromise on leadership is the most suicidal act a church can commit."[1] The elder selection is in place, in part, to help ensure that churches are not committing suicide because they have failed to place the right men in leadership. One element that will be clear in this entire project is that the process can begin with a man saying he wants to become an elder, or it can begin with the congregation approaching a man about becoming an elder. However, at some point, both the candidate and the congregation will be convinced by the Holy Spirit that this is a match that has been ordained by God.

This chapter will examine the process from the prospective elder's perspective. A church should desire that the prospective elder would communicate what God is doing in his life and heart that is encouraging him to seek the position of elder. This is a chance for him to express his heart and to express the work that God has been doing in his life to get him to this point.

---

[1] Charles Spurgeon, "This Must Be A Soldiers Battle," *The Sword and the Trowel.* (December 1889), 634

In order for a man to be considered for the office of elder, we must gain some information from him about his call, his family, his service in church up to this point, and his reputation outside of church. This first analysis is an opportunity for him to provide us with some necessary information to begin the evaluation process. If a man is unwilling to provide the information that is being sought, that should raise red flags and should eliminate him from consideration of the position of elder. The categories and questions sought in this section are certainly not the only questions that can be asked, but for us, they provided a well-rounded glimpse into the personal evaluation of the prospective elder.

The prospective elder's calling and character

As was mentioned above, the elder's call is essential to the overall process of selecting a man as elder. He must be able to show that he has a desire to serve in this capacity of elder. Therefore, he needs to show that his desire or calling is truly Spirit-led and not somehow coerced or manipulated by someone else. Failure to verify a man's desire to be an elder will only mean frustration, burnout, and possible heartache for all of those involved in the entirety of this situation. It will also mean that there was a failure to account for the statement in I Timothy 3:1 "The saying is trustworthy: If anyone aspires to the office of overseer, he desires a noble task".

The first "requirement" of an elder given in I Timothy 3 is that they desire the office of elder. This means that they must have a calling from God that He works in their lives and in the lives of others to communicate to him that he is in fact being chosen by God to serve as an elder. The call for the elder is two-fold: there is a personal, internal calling and there is a public or external calling that will confirm or affirm the internal call.

24

The Internal Confirmation of the Call

When we think of the elder's call, we have to think first of all about what God is doing on the inside of the man. In other words, there will be a sense within the man that causes him to realize that God is working on him and he needs to pursue the possibility of being an elder. This calling can be subtle for the man, taking years for him to personally realize, or it can be loud or obvious to him, coming on somewhat quickly if he has never really thought much about it. Ultimately, his calling is something that he cannot escape.

His call is an aspiration – I Timothy 3:1. Richard L. Mayhue has properly stated, "A man must sense the calling of God as a consuming desire in his heart."[2] The beginning point of the elder selection process has to begin with the prospective elder being able to communicate his burning desire to serve in this capacity. This burning desire means that it is a desire that he cannot escape. The Greek word here is the word, ὀρέγω and literally means "to stretch out especially with the hands, to snatch."[3] This indicates that the man who is being considered for elder cannot help but be an elder. This is not a passing desire that comes and then goes; this is a desire, an aspiration that the man cannot escape. It is the constant gnawing in his heart that this is what God wants him to do. This desire is inescapable and the man of God who is being called to be an elder will continually seek to do what is biblically necessary to be an elder.

His call is noble – I Timothy 3:2. Paul tells Timothy in this passage that the man, who desires the office of elder, desires a noble task. The word noble is the word that communicates

---

[2]Richard L. Mayhue, "Editorial," *Master's Seminary Journal* 6, no. 1 (1995): 2. Mayhue states as well, "The pastorate is calling to men who have a passionate desire to minister. He is not fit for ministry if he has not sensed the call or if sin in his life is muffling that call."
[3]Spiros Zodhiates, *The Complete Word Study Dictionary: New Testament* (Chattanooga, TN: AMG Publishers, 2000).

that this is an "excellent choice,"[4] a noble calling or a noble office to pursue. In other words, if a man desires to be an elder, this is a good thing. There are lots of jobs and careers that are not good or beneficial or noble. However, Paul makes it clear that the office of elder is a good thing. Therefore, the desire to be an elder and the realization of that desire as seen in serving in the office of elder, should be an exciting and valued position for that man. The opportunity to serve Christ's church as an elder is a privilege. This opportunity should not be taken lightly, but rather should be esteemed by those in whom God has placed this burning desire.

His call is Spirit-led – I Peter 5:2. We have examined the first two aspects of the man's call from I Timothy 3. However, there is one other passage that helps speak to the man's calling. In I Peter 5:1-4, Peter addresses the matter of elder in a clear, succinct manner. This particular aspect is taken from I Peter 5:2 "Shepherd the flock of God that is among you, exercising oversight, not under compulsion, but willingly, as God would have you."

There are three words of significance in this thought as Peter presents it. The first is that he is not to shepherd under compulsion. Compulsion would mean that he is not to be manipulated or somehow coerced or even talked into serving. Peter states as well that he is to serve willingly and eagerly. This means that this is something he is excited to do and something that he can't help but to do. The man who is truly Spirit-led will not be able to resist the call of God on his life to serve in this capacity, and serving as elder will be something he enjoys and continually desires to do. As Hiebert states, "He should not occupy the office as a reluctant draftee, doing an irksome task

---

[4] ibid

26

because he feels he cannot escape it."[5] God's desire is that those who are elders in the church are serving because of the leading of God in their life. An elder who is serving for the right reasons is a man who evidences the leading of the Holy Spirit on his life.

Peter goes on to state that he is not to domineer over those who are under his care. He is not to lord his position over them in order to get them to do what he wants them to do. The position of elder is a privileged position. If a man is not Spirit-led, he can easily allow his flesh to dominate over those whom God has called Him to lead. In order to prevent this, Peter says that the elders are to serve others as examples. The word that he uses here means to repeatedly strike or to blow. Peter is not saying that the elder is to strike or hit the sheep, rather the picture here is that the elder, like a mold, is to allow Jesus to stamp His image on him. Just like the songwriter stated, "Stamp Thine own image, deep on my heart."

The External Confirmation of the Call

When we talk about the external confirmation of a man's calling to the office of elder, we are talking about the fact that other people recognize that he possesses the qualities, desires and gifts necessary to effectively elder or shepherd the flock. This may be as simple as he can speak well and communicate God's Word well. It can be more detailed in how he functions as a shepherd and as an overseer, without having the title or position of elder.

When it comes to confirming a man's call to elder, it does not have to begin with the man himself, although, it has to ultimately include the personal, internal calling for that man.

---

[5]D. Edmond Hiebert, "Selected Studies from I Peter. Part 4: Counsel for Christ's Under-Shepherds: An Exposition of I Peter 5:1-4," *Bibliotheca Sacra* 139, no. 556 (1982): 335.

However, whether it is obvious to him that God is working in his heart yet or not, people who are watching this man should be able to look at the biblical aspect of being an elder and say that they see him as an elder. They see that he demonstrates and exhibits the necessary qualities in his life that would allow him to be an elder in a church. Sometimes, it is the encouraging words of those who are watching this man that gives him the confidence or assurance that in fact God is working in his life to have him be an elder, and therefore encourages him to follow through in the elder selection process.

The external confirmation from those who know the elder will not only help to encourage him, but it will also lend credibility to those who will eventually submit to his leadership and authority as an elder. As these people watch the potential candidate go through the elder selection process, it will reinforce their God-given affirmations that this man should serve as an elder.

God will ultimately work the calling of the man out, so that both parties either recognize that this man is called or that he is not called. God is not a God of confusion. If you have a man who believes he is called to be an elder, but those who know him and observe him do not sense the same calling in his life, then he is not ready to be an elder. On the converse, if a group of people think that a man is called to be an elder, but God has not given him peace and assurance and a calling/desire to be an elder, then he is not an elder. God will, in His great providence, align these two groups together. The internal personal call of the man will coincide with the confirmation by those who know him. To short cut this process and remove one from the other, is to do a serious disservice to the man and to the body of believers.

It would be best here to ask the prospective elder to communicate that, allowing for the fact that no one is perfect and that he desires a right relationship with God, he fits the character qualifications as given in I Timothy 3 and Titus 1. Again, if he is aware of something that would disqualify him, this would be an excellent time for him to reveal that and to bow out of consideration as an elder. Failure for him to do that will have devastating effects on himself and on the church.

The Prospective Elder's response if not selected

One of the possibilities that exists in a process such as this is that a man could get into the process and then have it discovered that he is in fact not ready or not called to be an elder. Just because a man *says* that he is ready or feels called does not in fact guarantee that he is ready to be an elder. Since this is the case, it is important for the current leadership, overseeing the process, to ensure that they communicate up front that it is a possibility that the man may not make it all the way through to becoming an elder. They also need to communicate that since this is the case, they would like to know how the man will respond if he is in fact not selected to be an elder.

The one challenge to the question at hand is that this is a hypothetical situation. "Hypothetically, let's assume you don't make it as an elder, what would you do"? The challenge comes in the form that it is really easy to answer with the right and biblical answer. If the man, for whatever reason, is not selected to become an elder and he does in fact respond properly (humbly, submissively, teachably) then that is a good indication that he would make a good elder some day when he is ready. However, if he is not selected to be an elder and he does not respond properly (blows his top, causes divisions, loses control) then this is a clear indication that he was not an elder and that the process worked in showing in some way that he was not ready to be an elder. This response process is crucial to giving a glimpse of who this man really is. It is easy to say the right things, but when you watch a man be slowed in the elder selection process or be outright denied going farther in the

29

process, you will be able to tell a lot about this man's true character.

The Prospective Elder's reason to be an elder

It is imperative that one of the questions that should be asked to a prospective elder is the question of why he wants to be an elder. Again, as with the hypothetical scenario above, it is possible that the man could answer with a Sunday school answer. However, the answer that the man gives should give an indication as to his intent and desire for why he is trying to go through this process.

If a man consistently talks about the calling of God on his life to serve in this way, or if he indicates that he is trying to glorify God by fulfilling the calling that God has placed on his life, then this is generally a good indication that he is pursuing this from a proper perspective. Even though these reasons could be just the man saying what he thinks people want to hear, it is usually a good indication of his desire for the position of elder from a humble and noble point of view.

If a man makes statements such as, "I have always wanted to be an elder" or "My dad was an elder and I want to be an elder to make him happy" or, "I want to be an elder to be able to take the church in a different direction" then these should be red flags on some level as the man is indicating that his desire to be an elder is not rooted in a call from God or even from the evidence that is seen by others in the church, but rather this desire is from some sort of personal agenda that he may have regardless of how needed a direction change there may be.

The prospective elder's functionality without the title

One of the things that are essential to look for in this selection process is the man who is functioning as an elder without having the position. Peter instructs us (I Peter 5:2-3) that the elder is not to lord his position over the sheep. One of the ways that this lording occurs is when a man relishes the title without the work or functionality of the role of elder. The man, who is greedy for the position and the authority that the position represents, to the neglect of living and functioning like a shepherd, is a man who not only will lord his position over the sheep, but also a man who is not qualified to be an elder.

Thinking back to the four men we described in chapter 1, are there any men that are in the position of elder just for the title or the positional authority? What is wrong when a man serves as elder with that attitude? What are the potential dangers for this man and the church when he serves as an elder without a God-given call or passion for being an elder?

A prospective elder must demonstrate that his desire is to function as an elder before he ever gets the title and the position. This means that he is a man who is actively building relationships with people, discipling people, teaching and instructing people, whether one on one or in a small group. The man who only wants to show up to a monthly elders meeting so that he can make decisions and in essence control the church, but does not disciple, build relationships, reach out to connect with new people and help to care for those in the church, is not in fact an elder. He is a decision-maker and a member of a board of directors, but he is not an elder. Many churches have men who are elders, who are simply in it for the power or control that that position offers. These types of men will have damaging effects on the church.

The prospective elder's family's commitment to eldership.

Several years ago, I counseled an older teenage girl who had witnessed devastating effects of her dad's moral failure in ministry. When I asked her whether or not she thought her dad was ever really qualified to be in ministry, she stated, "NO!" To this answer she responded that she knew things that were happening in the home that no one outside of the home knew. She said that she wished someone had asked her whether or not her dad was qualified to be an elder, because she felt that she would have said that he was not. Similarly, I counseled a woman whose husband had served as an elder of a church in the past. The wife stated that she knew that her husband had been unfaithful to her and was involved in sin at the time of being an elder. However, since no one had bothered to check with her on whether or not her husband was qualified, or if she was supportive of his decision to be an elder, she simply went along with it and now lived with regret that she had not said anything to someone.

With this in mind, it is extremely important to check with the wife and children, assuming they are of adequate age to know, whether or not they are in agreement of their husband or father being an elder and whether or not there are things that are happening at home that would disqualify him. Too many times, the position of elder is seen as a status symbol that must mean that if he has the position then the man is spiritual. Nothing could be farther from the truth. If a man is trying to be an elder so that other people think of him as spiritual, then he is trying to be an elder for the wrong reasons. A man must be qualified first before he becomes an elder. It must never be the case that he tries to become an elder to somehow justify that he is spiritual or to have other people perceive him as such.

Having the wife's support is going to be essential for the prospective elder as he serves in that capacity. If she is not supportive of his decision to serve as elder or if she has reservations about his qualification to be an elder, that is something that must be addressed by this man and the other elders who are overseeing this process. If a man and his wife are not in agreement with his serving as an elder, then he is not qualified to serve in that capacity. God will give both of them the peace that they need as they seek to discern God's will in serving.

The Prospective elder's commitment to the time requirements

It is the responsibility of the lead pastor or the current elders, assuming they are biblically qualified men, to communicate to the prospective elder how much time he can expect to invest on a regular basis as an unpaid elder. It is essential that there be open transparency and communication in this process. It is not right for the elders overseeing the process to sell the prospective elder with false concepts of the expectation of the eldership. There is no other way to communicate this thought, than to say, being an elder will be one of the most spiritually challenging things you can do. Not only will the demands on your time and energy be great, but your demands on your family will be great. Combine this with the fact that Satan would like nothing more than to destroy you and your family! Becoming an elder is a big deal and there must be open and honest communication of the expectations and demands that the elder will face as he fills this role.

Failure to communicate how much time will be expected from a lay elder will not only lead to frustration on his part, but also on the part of his family, and on the part of the church. Whatever you decide is necessary for the church situation you have and whatever you deem appropriate for the balance of life for the elder is entirely up to you and the needs of the congregation. However, failure to communicate expectations up front is not only rude, but it is also unethical, manipulative, and destructive to the body as a whole.

It is imperative that this not only be communicated up front, but also that the current elders do their best to hold each other accountable in how much time and energy they are investing as elders. Certainly, no one elder is in entirely the same life situation as any of the other elders. Some may be retired and have more time on their hands, while others may be young men with young families and demanding jobs. It is perfectly all right to even have different expectations for different men depending upon their life situation. The elders must be sensitive to this and be willing to pick up more slack as they can to help those who are needing some extra time for family or work.

The prospective elder's personal contacts for references outside of the church.

Paul makes it abundantly clear in I Timothy 3:7 that the elder must have a "certifying" testimony from those who are without the church. "Moreover, he must be well thought of by outsiders, so that he may not fall into disgrace, into a snare of the devil." In the informal survey that was conducted, only 10% of the churches that were surveyed, actually asked for references from those outside of the church. Clearly, there is a disconnect between what churches do and what I Timothy 3:7 says. Therefore, we have a place reserved for the prospective elder to give us the names of those who are saved and those who are not saved that we can contact, in order to find out how the prospective elder lives and how the unsaved community views him.

We will talk more about this in chapter three, but for right now, as we examine the personal evaluation section, we would say that this is an opportunity for the prospective elder to give us the names of several people who would be able to testify to his character and lifestyle outside the church. Again, it must be reiterated that if there is a failure to secure testimony regarding the prospective elder from those who are outside the church, then there is a failure to fulfill the biblical requirements of the elder selection process.

Now that we have examined the personal evaluation process for the prospective elder, we need to continue on in the process and examine further this matter of a certifying testimony of those who are outside the church.

3

Survey Says......

The Role of "a good relationship with outsiders"

Mark was an excellent Bible teacher! His class was the popular Sunday school class. When it came time for Mark to become an elder, his popularity propelled him to the position of elder very quickly. Unfortunately, since Mark was so popular and such a good teacher, the church that he attended did not deem it necessary to check with those unbelievers outside the church who could have testified to Mark's character. While he was winning friends at church with his charismatic personality, he was also displaying his charismatic personality in the workforce and was anything but trustworthy. In fact that realization came to fruition when Mark was arrested for embezzlement in his company.

Gene is another example of what happens when churches fail to ask for a certifying testimony from those who are outside the church. Never mind that he was a ladies man at work. Never mind that he had a wandering eye for women. The church was desperate for elders, and Gene seemed to be a great father and husband to his wife and kids. It would have been almost inconceivable to think that Gene wasn't faithful to his wife. No, he never knowingly had an affair with a woman, but he certainly was interested in checking out women as much as he could, and the men he worked with knew that. The church needed a man like Gene, at least the Gene they thought they knew. So the congregation put him in as an elder and did not bother to check with any of his co-workers on how he was in his character.

Unfortunately, these stories are not unfamiliar when it comes to church leadership. Pragmatism sets in and it becomes all too easy to fill a spot for elder. This is why in Philippians 2:15, Paul instructs the church at Philippi to ensure that they have a good testimony among those who are outside the church. Paul uses several phrases to indicate the challenges and the practical relationship between believers and unbelievers:

This world is crooked and twisted. If we said this in modern vernacular it would be, "the world is messed up!" Not only is it messed up, it is not in the process of being fixed nor does it want to be fixed. The two words that Paul uses are *skolios* which means crooked or warped (where we get the English word for scoliosis which is a twisting of the spine) and then *diastrepho* which means to be led away or turned away. The unsaved world is depraved. They are wicked. They are set in rebellion against God. In short, they are enemies of God.

Believers are to be blameless, innocent, and without blemish. In direct contrast to the crooked world, believers are to be characterized completely differently than the world. Believers are to be blameless. This means that it is impossible to find fault with them. Believers are to be innocent. This means that they are to be pure or untainted. In other words, they are to be people who live in light of God's holiness. This does not mean perfection, nor does it mean that they act like they are better than others. But it does mean that they are not duplicitous in their behavior. They are consistent in how they live. Finally, Paul says that they are to be without blemish. This means that they are to be morally blameless. Nothing sticks to them when it comes to their character. The unsaved world can say a lot about them, but they must not be able to say that the believer is characterized by immorality, profanity, a lack of integrity, or anything else that would mar his character.

Believers are to shine as lights in this world. So not only are believers supposed to contrast the crooked and twisted character of the world, they are supposed to shine as lights in the midst of that crooked and twisted world. The thought behind shining as lights is this: the world is so dark and so depraved that even though believers are clearly imperfect, their character and their lives which reflect Christ are to be so bright that they radiate in the midst of utter darkness. Paul was not calling for perfection or for putting on a show, but he was calling them to live their lives in such a way that they brighten the darkness of the world.

As we think about elders then, the prospective elder will be one who is so committed to the gospel. He will be so committed to Christ that that commitment will dominate his life in such a way that he shines as light in the dark world because of his commitment to being blameless, innocent, and without blemish. Again, this does not mean that he is perfect, but it does mean that he is committed unwaveringly to Christ.

As the church then determines what men they believe to be elders, the church must show due diligence in finding out various aspects of the believers relationship and interaction with those in the world. That is why Paul instructs Timothy in I Timothy 3:7 to make sure that the prospective elders have a good relationship with outsiders.

What exactly does it mean to have a good relationship with outsiders? The heart of what Paul is communicating to Timothy here is that Timothy is to ensure that those who would be elders must be respectable in the unsaved world. They must have a reputation that speaks for itself. This does not necessarily mean that the unsaved world loves this guy, but it does mean that at the end of the day, his life is consistent with what they perceive to be a Christian.

When I was in college, I worked for a large corporation in their warehouse and was surrounded by many men who were my age. They knew what I was studying in school and they were aware that I was a Christian. If you would have asked each one of them what a believer was to act like and be like, they would have had no issue telling you. In that scenario, the church that I attended at the time should have been able to ask any one of them how my life at work compared to the life of a believer. They should have been able to give a sufficient analysis of whether or not my life matched up with what the perceived life of the believer should be.

This is what Paul is saying to Timothy. The prospective elder's relationship with unsaved people is to be examined. The issue that Paul addresses is that the prospective elder is to be building relationships and have good relationships with those who are outside the church. The word outside is the Greek word ἔξωθεν and means "from outside: a person who is not a member of a particular in-group."[6] The prospective elder is to be engaged with those who are not a part of the church. This is not speaking about a local church, but rather, it is speaking about the church as a whole. This is someone who is not a part of the Kingdom. This is not speaking about someone who attends another church down the road, but rather someone who is outside of Christianity.

The believer's relationships must be good. Literally, Paul is stating that the character of the elder, his life testimony, must be certifiable. In other words there must be a quantifiable aspect as to how the prospective elder is doing in his relationships with unbelievers. The reason for this is really two-fold. First, it is necessary because it is possible that the church may have a skewed view of the prospective elder and they need to make

---

[6] Johannes P. Louw and Eugene Albert Nida, *Greek-English Lexicon of the New Testament: Based on Semantic Domains* (New York: United Bible Societies, 1996), 121.

sure that what he says and does in the church matches what he says and does outside the church. Just like the examples of Gene and Mark from above, it is quite possible that a man can be a two-faced person. They can behave one way around church people and behave entirely differently when they are not around the people they know at church.

The second reason for this is that it is necessary to certify his testimony so that the church can continually evaluate how they are doing in engaging the unbelievers. The biblical principle is clear from John 17:14-15 that we are in the world, but we are not of the world. The context bears light on the fact that we are to be engaged with those in the world. However, we are to be lights in the world since we are not part of this world, but rather, we are part of God's kingdom. As we certify the testimony and relationships of prospective elders we discover not only how well he is doing in engaging the world, but also how the world continues to change and how he need to continue to engage the world.

Paul comments as well that this is done in order that he does not fall into disgrace, into a snare of the devil. The real question here seems to be how does a man's relationship with the world and his being certified by the church keep him from falling into disgrace and into a snare of the devil? What is Paul communicating here that helps us to understand the context of this statement?

The man who has a good reputation among the unsaved is a man who is demonstrating spiritual maturity. He is a man who is not easily swayed or blown about by every belief or every temptation. He is a man who has been rooted and grounded in God's word to know how to handle the difficult situations of life and the difficult situations that present themselves with unsaved people. The temptations and the challenges that exist in the secular world are real and they are difficult. I know that when I worked at the warehouse loading trucks, barely a week went by that I was not offered to be treated to any type of sin I wanted to indulge in. The opportunity my unsaved co-workers saw in being the one to "get the Christian guy to sin" was real and it was strong. Almost nightly I was challenged with theological or doctrinal questions and scenarios. In this type of environment a spiritually immature person will easily be swallowed up.

It is interesting to note that Paul uses the word moreover, when he speaks of the testimony that a prospective elder is to have with outsiders. The moreover ties into verse 6 which speaks of his not being proud or arrogant. In addition to not being full of himself, he must have a good reputation with unbelievers. The proud, arrogant, pompous immature believer will fall into a snare and will be a disgrace to the cause of Christ. If a church does no due diligence in checking the testimony of a prospective elder with the unsaved people he engages with regularly, then they are putting into place a situation where this man will fall into sin and will bring a devastating blight on the church and on the cause of Christ.

The actual checking of these references can be a bit tricky. You are asking the unsaved friends, neighbors, or co-workers of the prospective elder to give you feedback on how these men handle themselves and interact with others outside the church. What worked well for us was having this communication done in an email that way, you can control the questions a bit more and you can also verify the feedback from the people you are asking to evaluate the elder.

Part of the challenge that a church needs to consider is that you are asking unsaved people to critique men who are saved. The possibility exists that they may be skewed or tainted in their responses. A church needs to be prepared to get an answer that may be snarky or resentful due to the fact that they may not appreciate what this man is doing in investing his life in the lives of unbelievers and sharing the gospel. However, our experience has been that even though they don't understand the role of elder or why the church is bothering with asking them questions, they typically have a relationship with the prospective elder that will allow them to at least be cordial in their response.

Here are a sample of questions that we asked people as we conducted this analysis.

1. How would you describe this man's character in light of his self-control?

2. How would you describe this man's character in light of being singularly focused on his wife (as opposed to being a womanizer)?

3. How would you describe this man's relationship with Christ?

4. How would you describe this man's character in light of his integrity?

5. How would you describe this man's character in light of keeping his cool in a difficult situation?

6. How would you describe this man's character in light of how he handles his children and his ability to keep them under control?

7. How would you describe this man's relationship with co-workers? Does he behave differently with saved people than he does with unsaved people?

8. How would you describe this man's overall attitude of life? Does he complain about everything or does he exhibit contentment?

9. From what you know of this man, is what he says he believes consistent with what he practices?

10. From what you know of this man, does he seem to be able to control the consumption of alcohol or is he someone who gets drunk?

To fail to check references of prospective elders from those who are unsaved is to fail in the elder selection process. To this end, there is not a magic number of references that must be obtained. For our case, we gathered at least two people who were saved, and at least two people who were not saved, to give us input on the prospective elder's character. We wanted to be able to see how the elder handled himself with both the saved and the unsaved. The stipulation was that these references could not attend our church that way we could get a better feel for how this man lived his life outside the church.

This self-evaluation process for the prospective candidate is an important step in finding out his heart and motives for wanting to be an elder. It gives insight into his willingness to commit to the rigors of being an elder and allows you to see his heart's desire for the position as well as his family's perspective on the matter. All of these are important elements as you begin to evaluate this man and his potential as an elder.

4

The Heart of the Matter....

Why doctrine is important?

In a very informal survey of over sixty churches, only 40% of the churches surveyed actually asked a prospective candidate for elder even one theological question. Even though this is clearly a miniscule amount of churches to have surveyed in the whole global scope, the fact is this: it is very possible that if you attend a church that has elders, then those elders may not have been tested doctrinally before becoming an elder.

In Titus 1:6-9, Paul tells Titus that he is to make sure that the elders are capable of teaching and defending God's word. If that is the case, and it is, then logic would dictate that the prospective elder has to be given an examination of his knowledge and understanding of God's word. In this section, we are not looking for a man who holds a Ph.D. in the Bible. We are looking for the man who is a student of God's word and who is capable of instructing others, He should be capable of defending the truths of God's word from those who would try to destroy it and lead people astray within the church.

These four sections below are a generic set of categories that our church used as we went through this process, these were areas we felt the prospective elder needed to have a grasp on in order to adequately teach and defend God's Word. You can look ahead to chapter ten at the end to see the entire list of questions that we asked the prospective candidate. Again, these are not inspired questions, but they will hopefully present an idea of the different questions that we asked. The framework for this section actually came from Littleton Bible Chapel in Littleton, CO, but was tweaked and adapted for our context.

The Prospective Elder and the Gospel

The gospel is central to everything in life. Those who are unsaved desperately need the gospel to transform their lives in justification. Those who are saved desperately need the gospel to continuously transform their lives in sanctification. The gospel is not just limited to evangelism. Therefore, since the elder is called upon to know and defend Scripture, he must be able to have a working knowledge of the gospel and its applicational truths in everyday life. Again, the questions that we asked are not exhaustive by any means. However, they do reflect a general working knowledge and comprehension of God's word and the good news contained in God's word. Failure to understand the gospel, on the part of the elder, will be devastating to his life and the life of the church. He will either lead the church into apostasy or legalism if he is not grounded in the truths and the application of the gospel for everyday life for every person.

The Prospective Elder and the Church

The church has always been under attack. From its inception in the book of Acts with the Judaizers, to its current war with culture, including the views of marriage and other socially charged attacks, the church has constantly fought to remain true to the text of Scripture and to the functionality intended within Scripture. To this end, the prospective elder needs to not only be cognizant of current and future attacks on the church, but he must also know how the church is to function within the biblical framework. The questions in this section are designed to gather a working understanding of the prospective elder's knowledge of the inner workings of the church, including its polity and the role of women in church. Again, much like the previous section on the gospel, a lack of knowledge about how the church should function, will lead to devastating results for that individual church.

The Prospective Elder and Lifestyle

How should a man, who is an elder, live his life? If one thing is clear, being in leadership brings scrutiny. There is no way to get around it. People will watch how a man lives, what he does, where he goes, what he says, etc… This is why Paul was so clear that a man's character had to be examined. But how far does that go? As with everything, the elder has to be sure that he lives within the bounds of Scripture. However, on the flip side, he has to know Scripture well enough to know that he does not have to conform to other people's standards.

Every person in a given church is going to have a varying opinion about some aspect of conduct. Some will not want the elder to drink alcohol, because they don't drink alcohol. Some people will not want him going to certain movies, because they don't go to those kinds of movies. Some will go so far as to say, it is okay for them to do something, but since he is in leadership as an elder, he can no longer do whatever activity they may be discussing. The challenge for the elder will come in knowing how his life is judged and how God, the righteous judge, expects him to live. The man who is not certain about this will not only begin to adopt other people's standards (whether strict or loose), but will potentially begin to impose those on the church in the decisions he makes as an elder. This is part of the reason why a man must show a level of spiritual maturity to not be tossed about by other people's opinions, convictions and standards.

The final section that we examined was the prospective elder's knowledge of general doctrine. These were doctrinal systems and beliefs that are crucial to the core of Scripture, but also ones that have been used to divide the church, as well. The elder needs to have a good working understanding of Scripture and the various challenges to Scripture that exist. Most of the questions asked in this section could consume volumes of books, as they have through church history. However, we wanted to know that the prospective elder has a good working understanding of the different questions and positions they represent, and that he has the ability to adequately state his position on the matter and support that position scripturally. Again, the prospective elder does not need to be a Ph.D. level academia; however, he does need to show that he can speak confidently to these particular matters.

The follow-up

Once a man has completed the answering of the doctrinal questions, we had him submit those answers back to the current elders for a follow-up interview. The purpose of this was to be able to give him an opportunity to defend or clarify any statements he had made in his doctrinal section.

The conviction that the elders bear responsibility for the oversight and the due diligence in the prospective candidates doctrinal position is inherently implied in I Timothy and Titus respectively. Titus 1 especially communicates the need for the current elders to be diligent in checking the doctrinal integrity of a prospective candidate. This is seen in the fact that the elders are responsible for not only teaching doctrine but also protecting the doctrinal purity of the church. One of the biggest ways the current elders do that is to confirm that the prospective elder not only knows Scripture, but is also fully capable of defending it.

In addition to the candidate's answers, we added any follow-up questions that the elders had in response to the candidate's answers. This all became part of the information that was granted to the church later for review. However, for this time, we added the follow-up questions and the candidate's responses into the doctrinal paper that he had submitted. In part this was to help show the congregation what questions had already been asked and what the response was in order to not repeat the questions when the candidate appeared in front of the congregation.

In the whole scheme of the elder selection process, this particular section is the most important section. This is not to negate in any way the importance of the other aspects. If a man does not have his theology together, he will be a danger to the church both in his inability to defend the church against those from the outside who would be false teachers and he would be a danger in that he could potentially teach false doctrine out of ignorance. The current elders must do due diligence in examining the prospective candidate for elder.

The Shepherding Philosophy

We had the prospective elder answer the four major categories of questions listed above. We then had him face a follow-up meeting to answer any questions that we had for him or clarifications we wanted him to make. Finally, we also asked him to write out for us a one to two page paper detailing his philosophy of shepherding.

We believe that the primary task of an elder is that he is to be a shepherd. We take this from Peter's writings in I Peter 5:1-4. The imperative command in this passage is to shepherd the flock of God that is among you. If the command for the elder is to shepherd the flock, then we believe it is absolutely imperative to have him articulate exactly how he intends to do that. We want to know how he defines shepherding and how he sees himself specifically fulfilling the role of a shepherd.

This is certainly not a requirement in the elder selection process and your church may decide not to have the prospective elder do this project. However, your congregation will fully embrace knowing how the man anticipates to shepherd them, how he has thought through the role of the shepherd, and what value he places on his role in being a shepherd. Scripture repeatedly makes reference to the shepherd and the sheep. Therefore, it makes perfect sense to have the prospective elder communicate his understanding of this role in his ministry.

Now that we have seen the personal evaluation and the doctrinal review, it is time to shift our attention to the role of the audience in the elder selection process.

5

The Ayes Have it....

The Role of the Congregation in the Selection Process

Up to this point in the process, we have examined the prospective elder's evaluation, his doctrine and his philosophy of shepherding. The elders have handled all of these matters, and to this point in the process, the congregation has had very little, if any, involvement. That is about to change.

There are two major philosophies of polity function within a church that uses elders. There is the elder-led church and there is the elder-rule church. The elder led church engages the congregation in actually voting on decisions in some matters. The elder-rule church typically does not involve the church in the voting process. If things are done well in an elder-rule church, the elders will solicit feedback and ask questions of the congregation so they know where the congregation is at on a matter. Although, as a general rule, the elders will make all decisions without the physical voting help of the congregation.

When it comes to the elder selection process, both types of churches—elder-rule and elder-led—must involve the congregation. Failure to do so is a failure to follow the biblical prescription of the elder selection process. Even though the elder rule church will not have the congregation vote on the prospective candidate, they must solicit feedback from the congregation on the man's character. How do we know this? We know from I Timothy 3 and Titus 1 that this man's character must be evaluated. That evaluation has to consist of more than just what is visible at church. The evaluation must consist of his home life, his leisure time, his work life, and all elements of his life that are able to be evaluated. There is no possibility that a current elder or group of current elders knows intimately how this man behaves and lives in all situations. Therefore, even the elder-rule church must solicit help and feedback from the congregation to evaluate whether he is above reproach or not.

So, what must the congregation evaluate? The following characteristics, which are found in I Timothy 3 and Titus 1 have been written about in several other books. We will not take time to exhaustively expound on them here, but we will briefly describe each character attribute so that those reading this can have a working knowledge of what the prospective elder is to be characterized by.

The Prospective Elder's Qualifications

The matter of the man's character is of upmost importance. The majority of the emphasis in Scripture on the elder is on his character. What kind of man is he? What kind of man is he when no one is watching? How does he interact with his wife or his kids? How does he interact with other people in society or at his workplace? These are important questions to ask. Since these characteristics are to be present in the prospective elder's life, they must be checked or verified by people in the church to ensure that these characteristics are actually present. Again, it is important to note that no one man should bear the responsibility for the entirety of the evaluation and assessment of the character of the prospective elder.

Judging a man's character can be a challenge. On the one hand, you want to be faithful to Scripture and faithful to the challenge to which Scripture calls us, to ensure that we in fact, have the right men serving as elders. However, due to subjectivity, we do not want to over-scrutinize to the point where no one is actually deemed qualified to serve as elder.

The overarching theme of this section will be that the elder is to be above reproach. This means that he does not have accusations that stick to him. In other words, he is not defined by anything other than consistent integrity. People who know him consistently view him as a solid, consistent, and reputable man. As Thabiti states in his book, "People would be shocked to hear this kind of man charged with such acts. Being above reproach does not mean that he maintains sinless perfection."[7] As Grudem so aptly states, "It is not optional that their lives be examples for others to follow; it is a requirement."[8] When we talk about each of the four main sections of the elder's qualifications, the consistent theme is being above reproach.

The Prospective Elder's Character

Matthew Henry stated that, "A man's character is not to be taken from a single act."[9] When we examine those men in Scripture whom God used mightily, men like David, Peter, Paul, and others, all of them have moral and character issues that, if viewed in a singular context, would eliminate them from service

---

[7]Thabiti Anyabwile, Finding Faithful Elders and Deacons (Wheaton, IL: Crossway, 2012), 57.

[8]Grudem, *Systematic Theology: An Introduction to Biblical Doctrine*, 916. Grudem goes on to state, "Those who are choosing elders in churches today would do well to look carefully at candidates in the light of these qualifications, and to look for these character traits and patterns of godly living rather than worldly achievement, fame, or success. Especially in churches in western industrial societies, there seems to be a tendency to think that success in the world of business (or law, or medicine, or government) is an indication of suitability for the office of elder, but this is not the teaching of the New Testament. It reminds us that elders are to be "examples to the flock" in their daily lives, and that would certainly include their own personal relationships with God in Bible reading, prayer, and worship."

[9]Matthew Henry, *Matthew Henry's Commentary on the Whole Bible: Complete and Unabridged in One Volume* (Peabody: Hendrickson, 1994), 663.

in many churches today. However, as God mercifully used these men and others, He certainly still mercifully uses all of us. None of us are exempt from blights on our record at one point or another in our life. Therefore, when we think about a man's character, it is best to do as Henry recommended and not look at single events in men's lives. Rather, we must look at the whole of their lives and examine the entirety of the man and his life.

Husband of one wife – I Tim. 3:2; Titus 1:6. When it comes to the issue of the elder being the husband of one wife, there has been several different opinions on this matter. Some argue that he cannot be divorced,[10] while others argue that divorce is permissible as long as it was under certain circumstances.[11] However, the issue here is not simply about whether or not he is married, or about polygamy, or about divorce. Rather, the issue is that the pastor/elder is a one-woman man. His entire devotion and focus sexually and emotionally is to be on his wife. He is to be singularly focused in a devout sexual manner to her. The logical application of this argument then, should be that even if a man is married and never has been divorced, he still could be considered disqualified if he is a womanizer or as Glasscock refers to it as a "playboy."[12] If he is someone who has a pattern and reputation of flirting with, or eyeing women other than his wife, this man is not the husband of one wife. This certainly does not negate or diminish the impact of divorce, but rather reveals that this man may not have committed the unpardonable sin as some people view it.

---

[10]H. L. Willmington, *Willmington's Bible Handbook* (Wheaton, IL: Tyndale House Publishers, 1997), 735.

[11]Andreas J. Köstenberger, "Hermeneutical and Exegetical Challenges in Interpreting the Pastoral Epistles", *Southern Baptist Journal of Theology Volume 7* 7, no. 3 (2003): 13.

[12]Ed Glasscock, "'The Husband of One Wife' requirement of I Timothy 3:2", *Bibliotheca Sacra* 140, no. 559 (1983): 249.

Yet, he may still be disqualified from being an elder (Eph. 5:31; Matt. 5:27-28).[13]

Sober-minded – I Tim. 3:2. In the book of Proverbs, Solomon states that the one who finds wisdom and understanding is blessed (3:13). When we think of the man who is sober-minded, we should think of a man who is watchful and circumspect. The word for sober-minded, νηφάλιος, would even be able to be rendered as, "one who always has a halter on himself."[14] The elder should be someone who is careful and one who does not rush into decisions. He is wise and understanding to the dangers of particular decisions. The elder is a man who watches where he is going and makes sure that he does not step in something that would be harmful or damaging to him or the church. The elder is not hasty or rash in his behavior and decision-making (Eph. 5:15-17). He is to "think rationally."[15]

Self-controlled – I Tim. 3:2; Titus 1:8. Self-control has been defined as, "physical and emotional self-mastery, particularly in situations of intense provocation or temptation."[16] The elder who is exercising self-control will be sensible and restrained in his behavior. He will restrain and keep under control all of his passions and his desires. He will be "level-headed."[17] He will not only follow the example of those who are more mature in their Christian walk, but he will also

---

[13]Douglas Mangum and E. Tod Twist, *1 Timothy*, ed. Douglas Mangum and Derek R. Brown, Lexham Bible Guide (Bellingham, WA: Lexham Press, 2013), 1 Ti 3:2–Tt 1:6.

[14]Johannes P. Louw and Eugene Albert Nida, *Greek-English Lexicon of the New Testament: Based on Semantic Domains* (New York: United Bible Societies, 1996), 751.

[15]Robert N. Wilkin, "The Epistle of Paul the Apostle to Titus," in *The Grace New Testament Commentary*, ed. Robert N. Wilkin (Denton, TX: Grace Evangelical Society, 2010), 1015.

[16]Martin H. Manser, *Dictionary of Bible Themes: The Accessible and Comprehensive Tool for Topical Studies* (London: Martin Manser, 2009).

[17]Roy B. Zuck, *A Biblical Theology of the New Testament*, electronic ed. (Chicago: Moody Press, 1994), 364.

make sure that he is an example to those who are following behind him. The challenge of "people-work" in ministry will test every elder at some point. However, the man who is self-controlled will, by God's Spirit and grace, pass each test (Titus 2:2,6).

Respectable – I Tim. 3:2; Titus 1:8 . The elder who is respectable is a man who is orderly.[18] The heart of this characteristic is how he lives his life and conducts himself. He is decent and put together. This includes his dress and his behavior. The reputable elder is one who lives with grace and demonstrates that grace and dignity to others. Respectable also bears with it the idea that one is disciplined in his life. This is not to say that he has to achieve a level of perfection or utmost organization and discipline, but his life should not be characterized as someone who is disheveled and sloppy (Eph. 4:29; I Peter 5:5).

Hospitable – I Tim. 3:2; Titus 1:8. The theme behind being hospitable really has the context of strangers, those whom we do not necessarily know, but we are willing to show love and help to. "We not only are to meet the needs of those people [strangers], believers and unbelievers, who come across our paths, but are to look for opportunities to help."[19] Being hospitable is also a willingness to open our homes and lives to others so all may see our spiritual character. There should be no hidden secrets with the elder. What you see at church should be what you see at his home and in his social life. At the heart of the matter of hospitality is relationship building. The elder will build relationships either in his house, someone else's house, or in some other location. The proper question to ask is "What kind

---

[18]Spiros Zodhiates, *The Complete Word Study Dictionary: New Testament.*

[19]John F. MacArthur Jr., *Romans*, MacArthur New Testament Commentary (Chicago: Moody Press, 1991).

of relationships is the elder building?" (I Peter 4:9; 3 John 5-8; Hebrews 13:2).

Able to teach – I Tim. 3:2; Titus 1:9. He possesses the ability to communicate the truths of God. This does not have to be in a public setting from a pulpit per se, but he must be able to diligently and faithfully teach and communicate the truths of God's word. The elder, when confronted with a biblical question, is a man who can take a person to the Scriptures to find the answer to the question that is being posed. He should be considered "apt to teach." He should be capable of conducting some sort of Biblical study or teaching whether that is one-on-one, in a small group setting or even in a preaching context in front of the entire congregation. Every elder is different in how comfortable they feel or how gifted they are in handling a large crowd in a public forum. However, all elders need to be able to adequately and faithfully share God's word with the sheep that they have been called to shepherd (Matthew 28:18-20; James 3:1; Titus 2:6-8).

Not a drunkard – I Tim. 3:3; Titus 1:7. The thought and idea behind this characteristic, is that the elder does not abuse or use alcohol incessantly. This is not forbidding elders to drink, but rather indicates that his life should not be characterized by one who is constantly drinking. [20] The issue of alcohol is controversial with some churches, and people, depending upon their various backgrounds and upbringings. [21] [22] [23] Sensitivity should be considered in this matter, but ultimately, Scripture

---

[20]Spiros Zodhiates, *The Complete Word Study Dictionary: New Testament.*

[21]Robert N. Wilkin, "The Epistle of Paul the Apostle to Titus," in *The Grace New Testament Commentary*, ed. Robert N. Wilkin (Denton, TX: Grace Evangelical Society, 2010), 1015.

[22]John MacArthur F., Jr, Richard Mayhue, and Robert Thomas L., *Rediscovering Pastoral Ministry: Shaping Contemporary Ministry with Biblical Mandates*, Electronic ed. (Dallas: Word Pub., 1995), 97.

[23]Knofel Staton, *Timothy–Philemon: Unlocking the Scriptures for You*, Standard Bible Studies (Cincinnati, OH: Standard, 1988), 75.

does not forbid the consumption of alcohol. The Bible, however, clearly forbids drunkenness. Therefore, to forbid the elder to drink in moderation, or to the point where he is not addicted to or dependent upon alcohol, seems to place restrictions upon him that Scripture does not place on him (Eph. 5:18). If an elder can't relax without a drink or he is reliant on alcohol as opposed to the Holy Spirit, then he should be deemed unqualified to be an elder.

Not violent, but gentle – I Tim. 3:3; Titus 1:7. The elder is not to be a bully or violent person; rather he is to be gentle or gracious and patient, long suffering.[24] The concept of the elder not being a bully indicates that he is to mirror or reflect the Great Shepherd. This means that he is gentle and caring for his sheep. The imagery seen in Psalm 23 should guide the elder in knowing how he should lead and guide the flock that is under his stewardship. Even though he may be tempted at times to beat the sheep he still responds with grace and tenderness as he gently guides the sheep that the Good Shepherd has entrusted to Him. This is why Peter refers to the Chief Shepherd rewarding those under-shepherds who lead and shepherd well (Galatians 5:22-26; Psalm 23).

Not quarrelsome – I Tim. 3:3. The elder is not to be known as a man who is given to conflicts, contentions, fights, or arguments. He is not to be combative with other people. Another way of describing this would be ornery.[25] An elder should have a gracious disposition and should be a man that attempts to live peaceably with others. The challenge for the elder comes in the fact that he is to be militantly defending the faith, the Word of God. Therefore, there may be times when it is necessary for the elder to be firm, resolved, and righteously

---

[24]Spiros Zodhiates, *The Complete Word Study Dictionary: New Testament.*

[25]Spiros Zodhiates, *The Complete Word Study Dictionary: New Testament.* ἄμαχος, "Not disposed to fight, not contentious or quarrelsome"

angry. A good balance to this is seen in Staton's remarks, "This does not mean that he will never engage in controversy, but he knows how to disagree agreeably. He knows what it means to have differences without animosities."[26] (II Timothy 2:22-26).

Not a lover of money – I Tim. 3:3; Titus 1:7. The elder who is serving the church as he should is not to serve the church for what he can get out of it financially. In other words, he is not to be greedy for money; he is not a financial con artist.[27] He is not to use the ministry as a means of extorting or scamming money from people. One of the challenges that exists today in light of the financial side of the elder and the ministry is the public perception that all pastors/elders are rich or are in the ministry for money. This is enforced by the health and wealth community of men who have gotten rich from the concepts promoted by the health and wealth gospel. The man of God is not in ministry so that he can use his position of power and influence to gain money through unethical or manipulative ways. Unfortunately, the list of those who have used the ministry for their own financial gain is long and it has left millions of people with negative concepts of those in ministry (I Timothy 6:9-10; Hebrews 13:5-6).

Not arrogant – Titus 1:7. When Paul tells Titus that the elder is not to be arrogant, it may be easy to think of this as someone who is haughty or full of himself. Although this is part of the idea that Paul is trying to communicate, the idea has to do with the fact that the elder is not a person who demands his own way.[28] He is not to be inconsiderate of others opinions or views. It means that he does not live his life consumed entirely with

---

[26]Staton, *Timothy–Philemon: Unlocking the Scriptures for You*, 75.

[27]Robert James Utley, *Paul's Fourth Missionary Journey: I Timothy, Titus, II Timothy*, vol. Volume 9, Study Guide Commentary Series (Marshall, Texas: Bible Lessons International, 2000), 44.

[28] Johannes P. Louw and Eugene Albert Nida, *Greek-English Lexicon of the New Testament: Based on Semantic Domains* (New York: United Bible Societies, 1996), 763.

himself. An elder, if he is functioning as he should, will be self-sacrificing for the flock that God has called him to oversee. This is the mirror concept of the Great Shepherd, Jesus Christ, who gave His life for the sheep. The elder certainly is not being asked to die per se, but he should be so focused on ministering to the needs of the congregation that he is not consumed with himself and his needs, views, or opinions. (John 13:14-17; Hebrews 10:24)

Not quick-tempered – Titus 1:7. Paul also tells Titus, that the elder is not to be quick-tempered. This means that he is not prone to angry outbursts; he is not a "hot-head".[29] If an elder is a "hot-head," then it is a good indication that he also struggles with being arrogant. His outbursts of anger or losing his temper are seemingly tied to his not getting his own way or not having things go the way he wanted them to. The elder is to be patient and self-sacrificing as he engages the flock that he is overseeing (Ephesians 4:25-27). There will be plenty of situations where an elder will have to put his own interests and preferences aside for others. If he cannot be humble and self-less then he does not image the Chief Shepherd.

A lover of good – Titus 1:8. We have talked repeatedly about how the elder is to reflect and mirror the Good Shepherd, Jesus Christ, as he leads the church in following Christ. James talks about the fact that God the Father is the one who gives good and perfect gifts (1:17). God is a benevolent God. The elder is a man who is also a lover of good. This means that he likes to be kind and do kind things for others. He loves benevolence. Beyond just loving benevolence and loving to see people have good things happen to them, he actually acts upon his feelings of kindness to others.[30] He is himself a giver of

---

[29] Johannes P. Louw and Eugene Albert Nida, *Greek-English Lexicon of the New Testament: Based on Semantic Domains*, 760.

[30] Spiros Zodhiates, *The Complete Word Study Dictionary: New Testament.* φιλάγαθος, means, "benevolent. Loving and practicing what is good (Titus 1:8).

benevolence. He blesses people as God blesses him. This may not always be financial, but it does mean that the elder will be a sharing man, who freely shares as God has freely shared with him (Galatians 6:10; I Timothy 6:17-19; James 1:17).

The Prospective Elder's Family

The clear analogy between the elder's ability to manage (steward) the church and his ability to manage (steward) his family is clearly spelled out in Scripture. Paul makes it clear that if a man cannot take care of his family, he cannot take care of the things of God, when it comes to church. Just as we have seen the value and necessity of a man's character being inline with the Scriptural expectations, so his family life must be inline with Scripture as well. It is essential to examine a man's family life as much as possible, to determine his capability of serving as an elder.

Part of the challenge that is present in this section, is to what extent the man's family is to be examined especially when it comes to his children. If a man has children who are married and on their own, do they still fall under the reputation of their father? Some argue that the behavior of older children does in fact affect their father's ability to be an elder.[31] Each church is going to have to wrestle through the extent to which they will apply a particular philosophy of an elder's children. For this section, we will be taking a general view of the man's children and will not be taking the view that his children have to be saved. Also, we will be taking the philosophy that says, when a

---

[31]John MacArthur Jr., ed., *The MacArthur Study Bible*, electronic ed. (Nashville, TN: Word Pub., 1997), 1885. MacArthur argues at this point in his study Bible, "'Faithful' is always used in the NT of believers and never for unbelievers, so this refers to children who have saving faith in Christ and reflect it in their conduct. Since 1 Tim. 3:4 requires children to be in submission, it may be directed at young children in the home, while this text looks at those who are older."

child is out from under the control of his parents, then his life is not necessarily to be a factor in the examination process of his father. This does not mean that his children's behavior does not matter. On the contrary, his children's lives are a huge consideration; however, we must also look at things biblically and not impose restrictions that Scripture does not impose.

His children are submissive – Titus 1:6. Scripture teaches that the elder's children, regardless of age, should have a healthy respect for, and relationship with their father. Those men who desire to be an elder are to be examples to others when it comes to their children. The difficulty is that not all children are sweet and perfect. Of course, none of them are that way, since they are all born as depraved sinners. However, an elder's children will have the characteristic that they submit to his authority and that they are obedient to his leadership. Even if a child or teenager of an elder is not saved, he should still conduct himself in an obedient manner and be submissive to what he expects them to do.

As an elder is being examined for his role in the church, his children need to be part of the equation of evaluation. If his children are un-submissive, in other words they do not fall under his leadership, then he should not be considered as an elder. If his children are not obedient to him, to the point where that is their consistent characteristic, then he should not be considered as an elder. If a man cannot lead his children and garner their respect so that they are willing to follow his leadership even to the extent of not being willing to obey him, then he is not to be considered qualified to be an elder.

His children are Faithful – Titus 1:6. As was examined in detail above in the footnote section, there are some who believe that a man who desires to be an elder must have children who are saved. Though I personally appreciate that sentiment, there is no way that you can certify the salvation experience of children. It is to this point that Strong's defines this word faithful in the following way: "worthy of belief, trust, or confidence."[32] The connotation seems to be more geared toward their overall behavior rather than the fact that they have made a specific profession of faith.

Another interesting note in the translation of this word *faithful,* is found in the KJV where it states that this means having faithful children, not accused of riot or unruly. Again, the behavior of the elder's children is important. It is vital to examine their behavior. Are they out of control? Are they known in the community as the terrors of the neighborhood? Are his children well behaved and respectful or are they living their life as they want with no regard for others around them? When it comes to evaluating older children, how they conduct themselves in attitude and action is crucial. No man should be considered an elder whose children are out of control in their behavior and interactions with others.

The Prospective Elder's Maturity

We have examined the elder's character and the character of his family. The attention now turns to his maturity or his level of spiritual growth. The elder is to be a man that exemplifies the life of a believer. This does not mean that he is perfect by any means. However, there are a couple of identifying marks that should characterize his life. These two particular marks must be taken into account. Again, like many of the other character traits, there is an aspect of subjectivity involved in each one of these areas as well. Some have discussed the difference between I Timothy (the church in Ephesus) and Titus (the church in Crete) for an explanation of why one passage contains this warning and the other passage does not.[33] However, when it

---

[32]Zodhiates, *The Complete Word Study Dictionary: New Testament*
[33]A. Boyd Luter, Jr., "New Testament Church Government: Fidelity or Flexibility," *Michigan Theological Journal* 2, no. 2 (1991): 132–133. The author argues accordingly, "In 1 Timothy 3:6 the phrase "not a new convert" (NASB; Gk. neophutos) is obviously a very important requirement for an overseer in the

comes to this man's maturity, it is essential that there be sufficient time to examine him and to see how he is growing in his relationship with Christ.

He is not a new convert – I Timothy 3:6. The prospective elder must have been saved for some time. Again, the question that naturally arises is how long is "some time"? "The idea within the imagery of this Greek term is "not newly planted."[34] Again, Scripture does not indicate a specific time frame, so a church must be careful not to impose a specific time frame on how soon after salvation a man can be considered for the office of elder. Certainly, if a church is so desperate that they are trying to rush a man into the office of elder, then there are probably other challenges and difficulties that are taking place in the church. Scripture states that the reason for not putting a new convert in the position of elder is that there is the real danger that he may be filled with pride. It is this pride that will lead to his falling to a point where he is no longer qualified as an elder and potentially will do damage to the body of Christ. The issue at stake here is whether or not he is mature enough to be an elder. If a church is examining this man in all of the other areas, he must be able to demonstrate significant spiritual growth in a number of important areas.

Ephesian church. The supporting explanation of the potential danger of conceit in the life of an immature leader (3:6) shows clearly why this qualification was included. However, there is not a comparable time/maturity requirement for the elder/overseer in Titus 1. What are we to make of this? Guthrie reasons that the "more recent establishment" of the Cretan church rendered such a longevity requirement "inappropriate." Kent expresses the same perspective in saying: 'The Ephesian church at this time had been in existence at least twelve years, and spiritually mature men could be found. In the case of Crete, such a qualification was not given (Titus 1) because it was apparently a new work and the ideal could not be insisted upon.'"

[34]Roy B. Zuck, *A Biblical Theology of the New Testament*, electronic ed. (Chicago: Moody Press, 1994), 364. The authors state, "The temptations to pride and self-deceit are too great. The possibility of a church's ministry being disrupted becomes more likely when a convert is elevated to a position of leadership too quickly. Leadership demands mentoring, and mentors earn the title by earning respect over a period of time."

It is perfectly fine to take your time with the elder selection process. This will help to reveal those who are not spiritually mature enough yet to be ready to serve as an elder. There is no set time on how long this process should take, but my recommendation would be that you allow this selection process to take close to a year that way you have the opportunity to observe the prospective candidate in many scenarios and reactions to ministry. Placing a new convert or even a spiritually immature man into the position of elder is very risky and potentially damaging to the body.

He Shows Marked Spiritual Progress – I Timothy 3:6. Paul warns Timothy in I Timothy 5:22 that he is to make sure that the church is not hasty in laying hands on men suddenly. This goes hand in hand with the admonition not to have a recent convert become an elder. The key for the church is to make sure that the elders that they choose are men who are growing spiritually and actively pursuing a relationship with Christ. These men should be setting an example for other believers of what it looks like to have a vibrant and active relationship with Christ. This is why Paul told Timothy that he should not be a detriment to the believers because of his age and his subsequent behavior (I Timothy 4:12). Men may be chosen to be an elder at a relatively younger age, but if they do that, they need to ensure that they are living as examples of what a godly man looks like prior to serving as an elder.

The Prospective Elder's Reputation

The final area of the elder's character and life that must be examined is his reputation. Specifically what is addressed is his reputation in the community. A man has to be able to have a reputation in the community that is consistent with the life of a believer. One of the challenges that presents itself in this area is that a man who lived an ungodly life in the public eye will have to spend some time out of the public setting, demonstrating the working of the Holy Spirit that is now present in his life.[35] This will be challenging for the man who is now saved and living in light his salvation. He will have to be careful that he evaluates the community that he once lived in as an unsaved man, and determine if he has adequately communicated the change in his life.

His Reputation Outside the Church – I Timothy 3:7. One of the challenges that a church body faces in the elder selection process is the fact that they may only get to see a man and how he lives one day a week. They may not see him the other six days a week, and they certainly may not see him as he interacts with co-workers or with his family and friends. This is part of the reason why a man must have his reputation checked from the community. If a man is living a hypocritical life, this will be revealed in this process. When you do due diligence to find out how this man is perceived and what testimony people have of him who do not go to church, you will find out the real character of this man.

The elder must have a good reputation with friends, co-workers, neighbors and any others who are outside the church. The word for outsider is *tón éxōthen*, and means: "from those that are without, or the strangers to the Christian community."[36] This word indicates those who are not Christians. Therefore, those who attend other churches must be asked about the

---

[35]John Peter Lange, Philip Schaff, and J. J. van Oosterzee, *A Commentary on the Holy Scriptures: 1 & 2 Timothy*, trans. E. A. Washburn and E. Harwood (Bellingham, WA: Logos Bible Software, 2008), 39. The authors state, "If before his nomination he had lived in gross sin, yet had been appointed, the remembrance of his old vices would still remain with those who had known him, and this might bring suspicion on the office itself. It was better for such a man, even after a genuine conversion, to retire into the seclusion of a private life, than take a prominent place. Otherwise he would fall εἰς ὀνειδισμόν—into suspicion,—whether deserved or not, and from those, too, within, as well as without the community; and thus, in his weakness and depression, he might readily fall into the snare of the devil."

[36]Zodhiates, *The Complete Word Study Dictionary: New Testament*

candidate and those who are not saved must be asked about the candidate. To know what an unbeliever thinks and perceives a believer to be can be a bit challenging, but the heart of the questions should revolve around his character and his functional interaction with those unbelievers in the community. I will say this though. The interview with the unsaved references will be a blessing to you if this man is truly a man of God. It is a thrill to hear unsaved people talk about him and his character.

His Effect on the Church – I Timothy 3:7. His reputation with unsaved people affects how the church is perceived and how influential it can be. His reputation with the unsaved also has bearing on how he handles himself and how Satan can affect him. The man's character must be evaluated so that he does not bring a bad reputation on the church. No one should be able to say, "Can you believe that that man is an elder at that church." The elder must ensure that his life and behavior inside the church matches his life and behavior outside the church. If he lives a double life, this will drastically impact the community's perspective of the church. This is why Matthew 5:14-16 talks about letting your light shine before those who are outside the church, so that God may be glorified.

The Congregation's Role

The next step in the elder selection process is to allow the congregation to evaluate and analyze the prospective candidate. Again, much like the need to acquire references and input from those without the church, the need to allow the congregation to take part in this process is just as crucial. When Paul communicates to Timothy and to Titus that they need to make sure that the potential elder has a good character, the implication was that they needed to do their homework, in order to ensure that he in fact was a man who had the integrity and character that Scripture required.

It is clear that this process of evaluation and selection is not dependent upon one person. The current elders will not necessarily know everything there is to know about the prospective elder. Therefore, they must reach out to the congregation who will collectively know him better than will one particular elder. The way the congregation is engaged in the process is somewhat subjective. This evaluation can be done in a series of small group meetings through the church, or it can be done as one collective gathering with a question and answer time. Evaluation can also be done by simply soliciting feedback from the congregation via surveys or mailers. Whatever the methodology implemented in this process, the crucial element is that the congregation is given a chance to give their feedback on the prospective elder's character.

The congregation must be instructed that what they are evaluating about the prospective elder is not simply a subjective analysis, but rather that they are evaluating a biblical analysis. In other words, as they evaluate this man's character and his family, and his maturity, and his reputation, they are analyzing this based upon Scripture. As was mentioned in chapter three, it is possible for churches to evaluate prospective elders on their own personal thoughts and ideas. In other words, "I don't like him as a person so I think he is disqualified." "He did something I didn't agree with several years ago, so I will hold that against him and therefore, he is not qualified." "He uses the KJV and I only use the ESV, so I do not think he is qualified." The examples could continue of course, but the point is that the elder selection process must not be based upon a person's own subjective view of someone else.

As we mentioned before, Strauch points out in his book, *Biblical Eldership*, that if there is one biblically disqualifying accusation against a man, then he is not to be chosen as an elder. This seems harsh, but this is in fact the proper biblical position on this matter. The requirements/qualifications of the elder are not a matter of getting a simple majority. They are all or nothing.

If a man is biblically unqualified in one area, then he must not become an elder until that matter is corrected. Too many churches have succumbed to pragmatics or to desperation and have allowed the belief that says, "we have to have elders" and as a result, they have dumbed-down, or simply overlooked particular qualifications in order to come up with men who would serve as an elder. This must not happen in a church. God desires that those who are responsible for leading the elder selection process have the integrity and fortitude to follow the biblical pattern and qualifications for the elder.

The congregation must examine the four major areas that we discussed earlier regarding the man's character. They must evaluate his character. They must be confident that his character is consistent with the testimony of Scripture. They must also evaluate his family. How does he interact with his children or with his wife? How does he handle the discipline and instruction of his children? The congregation must also evaluate his maturity. This is important, as the congregation is to ensure that the prospective elder is in fact spiritually mature. The congregation must also evaluate his reputation. Does the prospective elder have the testimony from those outside the church that he should have? To fail to do this is to fail in the elder selection process.

The congregation and the leadership together bear the responsibility in the matter of the elder selection process. Both must function together to faithfully commit themselves to doing the hard work of finding men who are qualified to serve as elders. If the congregation and leadership does the due diligence necessary, and the church discovers that they do not in fact have men who are qualified to be elders, then this has exposed to the leadership that they need to do the hard work of not only evangelization, but more importantly of discipleship, teaching, and training. It has also exposed to the congregation that they need to be attentive to the leading of the Holy Spirit in their lives. If God is in fact calling some of the men to be elders and they are not following God's leading, this is just as serious a matter as if the church had dumbed-down the qualifications to find men who in fact were not qualified.

If the congregation (even as simple as one person) does in fact have biblically disqualifying information regarding the prospective elder, they need to share that information with the leadership so that the accusations can be verified. Paul states that an accusation against an elder should not be received unless there are two or three witnesses (I Timothy 5:19). Therefore, it is perfectly reasonable that the accusation be something that can be verified by more than one person. If it is not possible to verify the accusation against the prospective elder from more than one source, then the accusation should not bear weight in the process. If, for some reason, this is an issue such as abuse, whether physical or sexual, then the proper authorities need to be notified and the process halted completely until it is resolved. This is the challenging aspect of the elder selection process. Dealing with possible accusations against a man's character is challenging to work through, but it is vitally important to the health of the church.

The Current Elder's Recommendation

The final evaluation is the elder evaluation and recommendation. This is where the elders, who have been a part of the oversight of the process, will examine all of the information. The personal evaluation, the doctrinal evaluation, and the congregational evaluation examine all of the feedback and information. If there are no accusations to be made against the man and the doctrinal and personal evaluations are acceptable, then that man should be put forth as an elder.

What happens next will be dependent on the particular polity of the church. Some churches are elder-rule. This means that although the congregation has a means to give input, they ultimately do not make decisions for the church. Therefore, the elders would then determine that the prospective elder is set to be an elder and he becomes one based upon their (the elders) approval. Other churches are congregationally engaged to the point that the congregation has a vote in decisions that are made. (The particulars of these two systems have been discussed in other publications and will not be examined here.) Once the information has been gathered by the elders and they have had a chance to fully examine the totality of information, then they will make a recommendation to the congregation.

The recommendation to the congregation, (assuming an elder-led polity) should be worded in such a way that states that this particular man has gone through the elder selection process and has passed all of the examination processes. The elders are recommending that he be confirmed as an elder by the congregation. The wording of the congregational ballot is important. It would not be appropriate to say, "Do you think this man should be an elder?" Nor would it be appropriate to say, "Do you want this man to be an elder?" Wording the ballot this way puts emphasis on the individual congregants personal opinion. This entire process has been structured to be as objective as possible. The ballot should be worded similar to this: "Based upon the totality of the information gathered in the elder selection process and according to I Timothy 3 and Titus 1, I confirm the leading of the elders that this man is a biblically qualified elder." This puts the onus on the Scriptural qualifications and removes the personal opinion of the congregants.

The impetus or driving force for the elder selection process is to be elder led. The current elders should be actively engaged in the oversight of the entire process for the prospective elder. In our case, we did not have any elders who had gone through any type of qualifying process. It was not possible to have elders who had not been biblically qualified try to take a prospective elder through a biblically qualifying process. For that reason, we decided to form a transition team that would oversee the process from start to finish. The team was made up of ordained men that we had both within and without the church.

If your church has not had biblically qualified elders before, and you currently have men serving as elders who have not gone through a process of proper evaluation, then it does not seem consistent with Scripture that these men should oversee this process. If you find yourself in this situation, it would be extremely advisable to form a team of ordained and biblically qualified men, either in your church or outside the church, who will be willing to help your church go through this process. These men should be men who have gone through some type of formal qualifying process such as what we have described here. Hopefully the current lead pastor of the church has been ordained, or at the very least was taken through an examining process in order to become the pastor of the church.

Since we believe in and practice plurality of eldership, then all of the elders, whether paid or not paid, must go through a qualifying process. To have men serve as elders, who have not gone through a formal qualifying process, alongside men who have gone through a qualifying process, is to strip the qualified men of their biblical authority and position. This process is challenging and can be sticky at times, as it was for us. Yet, by God's grace, it is possible to work through a process whereby the men who serve as elders are put through a biblically qualifying process.

6

The Big Picture...

Seeing the entirety of the process

This chapter is intentionally short. It is designed to be a transition between the process and the practical training and implementation chapters to follow. It is essential to not only review the material so far, but also to provide a brief synopsis of the process.

Step One – Personal Evaluation

The prospective candidate will take this time to inform us of his desire, family agreement, and self-evaluation for the role of elder. This is his personal assessment in communicating why he feels called to be an elder and that he understands what exactly he is committing to as an elder.

Step Two – Doctrinal Questionnaire and Shepherding Philosophy

The prospective candidate will take this time to write out his doctrinal position and philosophy on several major areas of doctrine, ecclesiology, the gospel, and lifestyle. This was done so that those evaluating him on his doctrine had a physical copy of his doctrinal answers and also so that we could make that available to the congregation. Though these four categories are not the only areas of evaluation, they provide a well-rounded insight into the heart, character, and philosophy of the prospective candidate. This is also the time for him to write out his philosophy of shepherding and how he intends to shepherd the flock that God has called him to shepherd.

Step Three – Follow-up to Doctrinal Questionnaire

This is the current elder's opportunity to interact with the candidate on his doctrine and his view of the various questions that were asked. This was an oral examination of his doctrinal answers. This also gives him the opportunity to answer any follow-up questions from the elders and allows them to probe deeper into what he believes and how his beliefs will be played out as an elder. The current elders should also follow up with him on his shepherding philosophy to make sure that he comprehends what a shepherd is and how that will be lived out as an elder in the church.

Step Four – Reference check

This is the opportunity for the current elders to check with the references that the prospective elder offered them of both the saved and unsaved people outside the church. This will allow the elders to see a glimpse of this man's character outside the church and to see if there are any red flags that may be present in the man's testimony from those outside the church. The elders doing the background check should be sure to be gracious yet firm as they seek to get the information necessary from the references. Understanding that some of these people are unsaved will be crucial as the elders communicate with them.

Step Five – Information Presentation to Congregation

This is the point at which all of the information gathered from the prospective candidate in steps one to four should be accumulated and presented in a packet of information to the congregation. This will be essential for the congregation to be able to see all of the information gathered up to this point from the prospective elder. This will help in the next step as well so that the congregation does not ask questions that have already been asked of the prospective candidate.

Step Six – Congregational Analysis

This is the opportunity for the congregation to be able to ask any questions of the prospective candidate as well. Again, your polity structure and how you view the role of the congregation in the decision-making process may affect how you have the congregation interact with the candidate. It is important to note, though, that the congregation needs to be involved in the process of evaluating the candidate. This can be done in several ways. You can do one big meeting with all of the congregation, you can do several small groups where the candidate spends time with various groups of the congregation for a more intimate feel, or you can offer that the candidate will be available for a Q and A time with anyone who is interested at a certain time and location. The congregation must be able to have a way to communicate back to the elders if there is any concern that they have. Again, even though he is not officially an elder, it is important to follow the principle of I Timothy 5:19. If someone does have a potentially disqualifying character issue, then there must be substantiation from two or three confirmed sources. This means that anonymous comments should not be admitted against the prospective elder.

Step Seven – Elder Analysis

This is the opportunity for the current elders to discuss the entirety of the information gleaned from the prospective candidate. The elders should evaluate the personal evaluation, doctrine, shepherding philosophy, references and the congregational feedback. The elders must take this time to evaluate all of the information and evaluate the man himself and his abilities as they have been observed over time at the church.

This is the time for the elders to determine if they believe this man is qualified to be an elder at the church.

Step Eight – Decision Regarding Prospective Elder

Depending upon the polity structure of the church, the decision of the elders may be the final decision point of the process. However, if the congregation is required to vote, then this is the time for the congregation to be presented with the elder's recommendation concerning this man. For instance, the elders would say, "we have evaluated this man, his character, his doctrine and philosophy as thoroughly as we could. We believe him to be qualified to serve as an elder." The decision is then officially given to the congregation to confirm. It is recommended that here, the congregation be asked to confirm that based upon the qualifications of I Timothy 3 and Titus 1 that they agree that this man is qualified to be an elder. They should not be asked if they want him to be an elder since being an elder is not a matter of popularity. Rather, it is a matter of character and philosophy based upon the Scriptural mandates for elders.

Step Nine – Installation of Elder

The final step in the process is that this man be officially installed as an elder. This can certainly happen any number of ways, but primarily, it should be something that occurs in a worship service in front of the congregation. The current leadership should be involved in somehow officially recognizing this man as an elder and that he should be given the respect of the position that is biblically warranted.

Since we have not discussed the installation up to this point, it should be noted that what the church is actually doing is officially recognizing the elder as a man who is licensed to Gospel ministry. This means that he is officially recognized by the State to marry people and is officially recognized as a minister of the gospel. For us, we presented each elder with an official document from the church that stated he was officially licensed for Gospel ministry.

The more you can help the congregation to see the official capacity these men now serve in, the more you will be able to function in a plurality/equality model. The congregation needs to see that these men have the biblical authority that they perceive the "Sr." Pastor to have.

7

Let the Fun Begin....

Teaching, Training, and Modeling Eldership

In Chapter 1, we gave the examples of Sam, Rick, Greg and Mike. Let's assume that these men are actually qualified to be elders and they have been newly chosen as elders. How should you go about teaching these men what it means to be an elder? How would you make it possible for them to experience the role of eldership as they try to get their feet wet? What books would you recommend that they read? Would you spend one on one time with them discipling and encouraging them as new elders?

Paul, in speaking to Timothy in II Timothy 2:2, makes it clear that the role of discipleship is a crucial part of the process in bringing along other men, specifically as we think of the elder context. If we desire to have men who not only know and defend God's Word, but also are capable of passing that on to other men, then we have to be engaged in the discipling or teaching and training process. Now that these prospective elders have been chosen, they are no longer prospective elders. They are elders. A church may decide to call them elder's elect or elders-in-training, but the heart of the matter is they are elders. Therefore, this training time is for these new elders.

Once the church has selected elders, it becomes easy to assume that the job is done and now we can let these men elder. However, things are really just getting going for these men and for the church. It cannot be emphasized enough that these men will need to be discipled and mentored even more than they have been as they enter this new role. Failure to continue to meet and disciple these men will lead to frustration, assumptions that they are functioning biblically, and ultimately to failure as they try to find their way in the role of elder.

In the context of training elders in the church, there is no specific process that must be followed. The training that we offer and provide for these men can be seen in several different categories. There is training by teaching, training by example, and training by practice. To be quite honest, any and all of these are excellent ways to train, teach, disciple, and encourage the man who is now an elder, however, he needs to be helped to know how to specifically function as an elder.

Training the New Elder by Teaching

It is entirely appropriate to have the new elder go through an organized or methodical teaching process for learning the role and functionality of being an elder. As we went through this process, to look at what training would be best, we identified five major areas that we wanted the new elders to be familiar with. The five areas were: plurality of eldership, eldership functionality, church philosophy, ministry life, and leadership selection. We felt that this was a balanced, well-rounded look at the whole of the ministry of church and leadership. We asked the elder to read one book from each category and then to give a one page or less synopsis of the book.

These five categories of training are what we felt were the backbone of being an elder. The first category of plurality was especially important for us. Our church for fifty plus years was a Baptistic model of a single authoritative leader. The church had men with the title elder serving around the Senior Pastor, but there was no real functioning of plurality and equality of leadership. Therefore, we knew that it was essential to do teaching and training in this area of plurality. This is why

77

Strauch's book on *Biblical Eldership* and Helleman's book on *Embracing Shared Leadership* were vital resources for us as we began to model the plurality of leadership. Again, this may be new to some of you or to your church, but these two books are excellent resources for you.

The next category we addressed in our training was that of elder functionality. We wanted to make sure that these men had a good working knowledge of how elders functioned. We did not just want to have men who gathered once a month to be decision-makers. Rather, we wanted men who would be actively engaged in the life of the sheep and that they would understand their role of being a pastor to the congregation God has called them to shepherd. This was a key element that was missing before, so to be able to take the new elders through this teaching was very important.

The third category of teaching was that of church philosophy. By this we mean, what is the goal and purpose of church? Why do we exist? What are supposed to be accomplishing? How do we fulfill this? We examined two different books, *The Trellis and the Vine* and *Total Church*. Both of these books are discipleship-based books that deal with how we live our lives as believers, both inside and outside the church. Both of these books are excellent resources for new elders who need to be grounded a bit more in the process of how church should work.

The fourth category we addressed in our teaching was the matter of ministry life. One of the big things we wanted to be careful of was to not only inform the elders of the pitfalls and dangers of ministry, but also to help them to be aware of the effects that ministry would have on their children and their wives. The demands of ministry can be difficult to handle, but if a man is not prepared for the realities of ministry and the various demands, there is a strong possibility they will succumb to the pressures and not be able to have the faithful, long-term ministry God would desire for them.

The fifth category we taught through was the leadership selection process. This was done specifically so we could ensure the continuation of the elder selection process and the deacon selection process, as well. We wanted to be sure that those in leadership after us were communicated with on the necessity of the selection process as well as the inner workings of the process. We wanted to make sure that the work and effort we had struggled through was able to be passed on to future generations of leaders. It is generally safe to assume that if a man has come through the process that we laid out, that he will see the importance of it. But, we wanted to be able to help him be able to facilitate the process as well.

Training the New Elder by Example

In addition to teaching the new elder with a methodical and intentional process, it would be great to engage him in training by example. This would entail allowing him to watch the other elders at work in the business of shepherding: taking him on calls, having him sit in on meetings with different leaders or other elders, having him watch and critique the "platform performance" of the other elders. Anything that you can do to allow the new elder to observe the current elders in their practical day-to-day role of being an elder will be helpful for him and for you as you seek to mentor him into this role. The more training and teaching he can have, the more likely he will be to succeed as an elder. It is the duty of the other elders to bring the new man along and help him as best they can to get adjusted and acclimated to the role of being an elder.

Modeling eldership can be intimidating. The expectations that the congregation places on you are challenging and of course, Satan is actively seeking to discourage you if not destroy you. However, as trust is built and as men learn to embrace their God-given role of elder, it becomes easier to allow yourself to be an example of an elder to others. Humility is the key to keeping yourself from being so full of yourself that you cannot function as an elder or be used to mentor and train others. Allowing yourself to be used by God to mentor another elder will be one of the most rewarding things you can do as you see God expanding the possibilities for the Kingdom in the life of another elder.

Training the New Elder by Practice

The third way to engage the new elder in the training process is by simply allowing him to get in to get his feet wet, so to speak. Often times, this is the best way to do things. If this man has gone through a qualifying process, then we can rest assured that he at least has the head knowledge of the elder's functional role. You need to be prepared for him to make mistakes and not know how to do everything, but you also do have to allow him the space he needs to become the elder that God wants him to become. If the existing elders choose to micromanage the new elder, this will only lead to frustration on his part and on the part of the congregation. This requires gracious patience, but with God's help, the new elder will be functioning well in a short amount of time.

There is certainly a fine balance that must exist in this training process. Too much too soon and the new elder may crash and burn. Too little too long and the new elder may grow frustrated and weary of waiting. Communication is key to making this relationship work well. Keep asking for feedback from him and the other elders to ensure that things are moving along at a comfortable pace for him and for the rest of the elders. It is exciting to watch God work in this process and to allow a man become the elder that God designed him to be.

The Training Process for New Elders

This is the list of books we gave to each candidate and had them choose which book from each category they wanted to read. For

each category listed below, please read at least **one** of the following books and write a synopsis of no more than one page

Plurality of Eldership

Biblical Eldership (Booklet) – Alexander Strauch
Embracing Shared Ministry – Joseph Helleman

Eldership Functionality

Church Elders – Jeramie Rinne
Elders in the Life of the Church – Phil Newton and Matt Schmucker

Church Philosophy

Total Church – Tim Chester and Steve Timmis
The Trellis and the Vine – Colin Marshall and Tony Payne

Ministry Life

Dangerous Calling – Paul David Tripp
Brothers, We Are Not Professionals – John Piper

Leadership Selection

Finding Faithful Elders and Deacons – Thabiti Anyabwile
40 Questions about Elders and Deacons – Benjamin Merkle

8

What to Expect When You Are Biblical

The results of the process in the church

This chapter will examine the results or the consequences of implementing a new model. If you have been a part of a church that has not had a biblical model of selecting elders then you potentially understand how unhealthy your church may be. Implementing a new model of elder selection will drastically impact your church. However, just because there is a new model in place does not necessarily mean that everything is magically better. There will, though, still be clear evidences of the work of God in the life of your church.

This chapter will examine some of the areas that you may potentially see changed as a result of the new model. We will examine the changes for the congregation and then changes for the leadership. There are other changes and blessings that may come as well, but we will focus on some of the areas we saw changed at our church. The change for the congregation and the change for the leadership certainly bear more weight in the matter, and examining the effects in these two areas will give a broad snapshot of the positive changes that came as a result of the new model. Again, no model is perfect and no church is perfect, but one thing remains clear: God blesses when churches and people do as He expects them to.

The Results for the Congregation

Whether or not the congregation ever expresses it, there is some sort of underlying angst that is present when a church does not have biblically qualified men in place as elders. Christ intends His church to function properly and that begins with the right men to serve as elders in the church. When that key element is missing, the congregation inherently cannot function as it should. Therefore, there is a problem that is unresolvable within the DNA of the congregation because the leadership is not functioning as it should. When you change the process of elder selection in the church to match the prescriptive plan of Scripture, you can expect some things to change for the congregation for the better. This change may take time and it may be painful at times, but change will occur nonetheless.

Qualified Leadership

It is important to note as we discuss this section that you may have had, in your church, men who were godly men who loved the Lord, yet were not called by God to be elders. When we say that a result of the elder selection process is that you now have qualified leadership, it should not be implied that the men who were in leadership before were some how ungodly men or men who did not love Christ. In fact, it is very possible that some of the men who were in leadership prior to the selection process being implemented may have been very godly men who were respectable men of character. However, as we have stated, if they are not called to be an elder or they have no desire to be an elder, then they should not be serving in that capacity. If they do serve as elders, no matter how godly they may seem, you will have challenges within the congregation. This is because these men are not elders and therefore will not lead the church, as Christ desires the church to be led.

Having qualified leadership for the congregation is like knowing that the man who is giving you medical advice and treatment has a board certification behind him to lend him credibility. This process gives a certifying confidence in the men that God has led to be an elder. The joy and the encouragement that the congregation receives as a result of the new process will be a privilege to watch and be a part of. Having men who were willing to go through and complete a qualifying process will provide the congregants of your church men they can follow, embrace and serve with heartily.

Active Shepherding

It is impossible for one man to effectively shepherd an entire congregation by himself. He must have the help of other shepherds to help him in this endeavor. In our case, it had never been expected that elders would actually shepherd the flock. Therefore, the responsibility fell to the lead pastor to shepherd. One of the blessings of having a biblical process for selecting men to be elders and having men who are called to be shepherds is that they have a desire to shepherd the flock along with the lead pastor.

Under the new model at our church, elders are expected to give an average of ten to fifteen hours a month in active elder care. Each church will have a different philosophy when it comes to their expectations of lay elders, but for us, we at least started with this amount, as this was a major increase in what had been expected of previous elders. A challenge that existed before the new model was expecting the elders to shepherd when they had no working knowledge, desire, or interest in shepherding. Under the new model, elders are not just expected to shepherd, but they are held accountable for their shepherding. This increase in active shepherding is not only noticed, but also appreciated by the congregation. The congregation's desire is to be taken care of as God intends. This is why elders are referred to as under-shepherds, and the congregation is referred to as sheep.

84

Vision for Future Gospel Growth

As part of the new model, the prospective elders are required to provide their vision and their goals for the church. As the Holy Spirit works in their hearts, they should be sensitive to the leading of the Lord and the vision and big picture plan they have for the church. This should align with the other God-called, biblically qualified men that they serve with. This allows the vision to be removed from one single man and placed upon a group of men who are called and qualified to be elders. These men will be sensitive to the leading of the Holy Spirit in their lives, as they lead the church that God has called them to lead.

Having a group of men who have vision, goals, and a humble desire to work together for the glory of God is a big deal for the congregation. The church has gone from having little if any vision to having a group of men who are sensitive to the leading of the Lord in their lives to communicate the vision that God has given to them as a whole. This vision and clear direction has been vital for the engagement of the church. It is this vision that has enabled the congregation to rally stronger around the elders and to have the energy, enthusiasm, and fortitude to engage themselves in the work of the ministry.

Allowing, or maybe we should say requiring, the men to communicate their vision for the church has been helpful in the elder selection process as the congregation gets a chance to examine where the prospective elder feels the Lord would have them go as a body. This is a great way to analyze whether or not the prospective elder has some type of agenda when it comes to leading the church in the direction that Christ desires. Though the exercise of communicating vision to the congregation may be a challenge for some prospective elders, it is a vital aspect of being an elder and communicating what the Lord is leading the prospective elder to do in terms of the church's future.

It has been stated and seemingly proven, that kids actually desire boundaries and discipline. The analogy here is not that the congregation is young or that they need to be disciplined, but rather, it can be said and seemingly proven as well, that the congregation embraces and seeks oversight. They desire a group of men who will work to protect them and guard them from the dangers that exist in the world today.

Scripture is complete with passages that address not only the presence of false teachers and wolves, but also the need to protect the flock from false teachers (Matt. 10:16; Acts 20:29;II Peter 2:1-3). When the elders are functioning as they should and they are proactively addressing matters of protection and help in the life and health of the church, the congregation will respond favorably.

The work of biblical oversight allows the congregation to do the work of the ministry that God has called them to, without fear of external or even internal threats. When elders are functioning as they should, they help the congregation to thrive in their role of serving and ministering. A church that does not provide proper biblical oversight will be a church that is constantly dealing with and addressing the consequences of that failed leadership. This lack of biblical oversight inhibits the health and productivity of the congregation, and it inhibits the church's ability to move forward effectively. The health of the church is the responsibility of the elders as they lead, teach, and exhort the congregation.

The Results for the Leadership

The consequences, or rewards if you will, for the congregation have been discussed and certainly they will be evident in the lives of the congregation. However, the leadership receives some blessings and rewards as well. This comes from the implementation of the new model for selecting elders. The relationship between the congregation and the leadership is a mutual relationship. When the leadership functions properly, the congregation begins to function properly. When the congregation functions properly, the leadership will reap benefits as well as they see the Spirit working in the life of the congregation.

Joyful Submission

We mentioned in the previous section that when the leadership is not biblically qualified, it will produce underlying angst within the congregation. Again, whether that is visible or not is different within each congregation. However, when there is that underlying angst, the congregation will typically struggle with their response to the leadership. Namely, they will struggle with joyfully submitting to the elders and to their leadership as they follow Christ's will for the church.

With the implementation of the new model of elder selection there should be a definite change that takes place in how the leadership is treated and how they are shown respect and appreciation. Part of this is seen in the fact that as elders go through the qualification process, they are naturally recognized as holding an authoritative position. There should be an increase in the congregation's comprehension and working application of a plurality of eldership.

This joyful submission is evident in the attitudes of the individual congregants toward the leadership, as well as in the personal interaction with the congregation and the leadership. This is not a magic pill that suddenly makes everyone sweet and kind. However, as a whole, the congregation will begin to realize that their God-given leadership is given to them for a purpose and that it is necessary to submit joyfully, and to graciously allow them to be led where God was leading. I imagine that as the elder selection process continues to play out in the years to come, the relationship between the congregation and the leadership of a particular church will continue to gel and mold in such a way that the two will be a formidable group as they minister together for the cause of Christ.

Renewed Enthusiasm

By far, the most noticeable change in the congregation, in terms of their relationship with the leadership, is the renewed enthusiasm that people have in general for the cause of Christ. This will be evident early on in the process, but especially at the congregational review of the prospective elder. The congregation will be excited to not only know that there is a process now for selecting elders, but also to realize that the new model is actually being followed through on and that they could have a part in the selection of the elders of the church.

The excitement that the new process will generate will be exciting to watch and yet, at the same time will provide more opportunity for teaching and instructing. The biblical concept of plurality is challenging for some to comprehend and grasp from a practical aspect, but as a whole, the entirety of the process allows for the congregation to be enthusiastically engaged in the life of the church and in their relationship with the leadership.

The excitement and enthusiasm that comes as a result of the new model is seen in how people interact with one another, as well as how they interact with the leadership. There is renewed hope and anticipation of what the future might hold now that the leadership of the church has been selected. The forward-looking results will be noticeable and more people will not only be equipped to do the work of the ministry, but they will also be more enthusiastically engaged in the work of the ministry. Certainly not everyone will have the same level of joy and excitement. No church is ever going to be perfect, but as a whole, the congregation will be increasingly enthusiastic about the future of the church.

Engaged Service

The previous change, renewed enthusiasm, goes directly hand in hand with the next blessing to the leadership. The leadership also receives the joy of seeing engaged service. Seemingly directly correlated to the renewed enthusiasm, the congregation will become much more engaged in serving in the church and serving in the community. Though some may have knowingly been cranky or perturbed by the leadership prior to the new selection process, many will have been generally frustrated with the leadership and the direction of the church. This results in many people leaving the church or if they do stay, they may have stayed with a bad attitude.

Having a congregation who begins to be engaged in serving and allowing their talents and abilities to be used is refreshing, and it is great to see so many people who will be willing to step up and be involved in so many different ministries. This is the heartbeat behind continuing to have renewed enthusiasm. It is often difficult to ascertain what causes what in church. However, it is clear that having proper leadership is definitely part of that equation. To be a part of a church movement that becomes enthusiastic about their engagement is exciting to watch. God truly is not dead, and He truly desires to see His church thrive. I am convinced that the impetus, in part, of this thriving, is to have a properly functioning selection process.

Renewed Confidence

The final blessing that can come to the leadership is a renewed confidence. Before the new process, there is sometimes little if any confidence in the leadership. In fact, most of the emphasis of leadership is placed upon the lead pastor. Many view the lay elders as rubber stamps for his agenda and his direction. The confidence and trust in the leadership is often minimal and unfortunately, as a result, many people wind up leaving or at the very least, being frustrated with the church.

Some of the congregation will not think much of their frustration and lack of confidence in the leadership. In their ignorance, they will not have noticed a lack of vision knowledge on how to handle a situation. However, with the new model and with new men leading the church, the congregation will be able to have the confidence in their leadership that God intended. The issue is not necessarily who is leading the church. It is very possible that the men who served before as lay elders were good men. The issue is whether or not the congregation can trust the process of how they became to be elders and can they trust these men in general to lead the church as Christ desired.

Having a congregation that has the confidence in you as a leader is exciting and thrilling on many levels. A lack of confidence is not helpful to either side. In fact, it is not just un-helpful, it is downright demoralizing. However, the new elders will be thrilled and can relish the fact that the congregation can be confident in their ability to lead as they are sensitive to God's leading. The relationship between the congregation and the leadership is as vital, in many ways, as the relationship between a husband and wife. The two must be able to work together to further the cause of Christ. By God's grace, your church has great potential to further the cause of Christ in the area where He has placed you around the world as you both seek to be sensitive to the Spirit's leading.

9

Enquiring Minds Want to Know

What to do in certain situations

The following scenarios are just different questions that you may have as you work through this process of eldership. If you are like me, you have lots of questions and often it is hard to know who to ask and what to ask. These scenarios are just a couple of things to consider in this process. Again, these are my suggestions as I have moved through this process myself. I trust that this information will be helpful and encouraging to you as you journey through this process.

What to do if you want to move your church to eldership?

This is a bigger question than can be answered here. Also, this question would assume that you are not a church plant and just haven't gotten to the point where you have elders. This question is assuming that your church has functioned with a strong single leader hierarchy type of polity. If you are in this type of single leader polity, however, this is certainly a viable question if you are in a church that does not currently have elders and you feel convicted by Scripture that a plurality of eldership is what you should do. I would offer a couple of different cautions in this process.

First of all, make sure that you do not violate some sort of ethical trust that was developed in your becoming the pastor of the church. For instance, let's assume you have come to the conclusion that the church needs to move to a more biblical model of eldership. If you have not discussed this with the current leadership and the congregation in the process of you becoming the Pastor, then you need to be extremely careful. You need to be sure that you did not accept the position, which by default said you agreed with their polity, in order to radically change things on the church once you arrived there. Now, if part of the discussion of you coming as pastor was that you would help change the church to an elder polity model, then have at it and make the changes necessary to get to where you want to be.

Second of all, I would say that you should be careful as well in this process of changing to a plurality of eldership to be sure that you give plenty of time for the congregation to adjust to the practical functionality of a plurality of eldership. If the congregation has been used to a single leader top-down model of polity, then they will not quickly adapt to a plurality model. It is one thing for them to agree to change the polity structure, but it is an entirely different thing for them to function as the congregation in the new model. The congregation will need time to understand that there is a group of men who are leading the church now as opposed to a single leader.

If you are convinced that you need to change the church to a plurality of eldership model, then I would strongly encourage you to visit Alex Strauch's website, www.biblicaleldership.com where you will find comprehensive resources and information on a step-by-step process of how to move the church body to a plurality of eldership model. Alex has spent the vast majority of his ministry life studying, teaching, and helping churches and pastors think through eldership.

What to do if your church does not have an elder selection process?

It is very possible that your church has elders, mostly in name or position, but not necessarily in function and it may not have an official process whereby the church can select men to be in that position. If that is the case, then you are in a similar situation that we found ourselves in at our church.

Implementation through Vision

Part of the process of implementing a change in the elder selection process is the establishment of a vision. It is clear that when a group, organization, or body of believers does not have a clear vision of where things are going and what needs to be accomplished, then there is an unhealthy and often stagnate environment. In order to combat that, and to provide clear direction and clear vision of not only what Scripture intended for the church, but also for the ability of the people to be able to move forward, we needed to communicate a clear vision to the people.

I took a Sunday morning and delivered a message with the following content. We had established three different aspects of our vision: Our vision of our leadership, our vision of the congregation, and our vision of the community. We wanted our elders, deacons, and the congregation to be functioning biblically. We believed, and actually have seen, that when all three groups are functioning biblically, then the body is healthy and the church can actually move forward for the cause of Christ.

It was clear that we needed to clearly communicate the vision for where we had been, why that had failed, where we intended to go, and how we planned to get there. It was this vision casting that enabled us to establish a framework that we could build the new process around.

Implementation Through Constitutional Change

In order to facilitate the changes necessary, we had to examine our constitution, which is our governing document. Obviously, God's word is our governing authority, but for sake of how we operate, the constitution is the guiding document. To this end, as we discovered that our constitution did not allow us to function as we should biblically, we had to do the right thing and make the necessary changes to the constitution that would align us with Scripture. The struggle was that the relationship between the congregation and the leadership was so strained that we had to work through the constitutional changes carefully. Therefore, as we progressed, we had to make changes in a stair-step fashion over a period of time. We examined and changed the following things.

The Elder Selection Policy. In order to begin the process of a new elder selection model, we needed to put in place a policy or manner of doing things that would give us the framework for how to select new elders. This was done prior to changing the constitution so that we could at least allow the process to start since, up to this point we did not have any type of formula or model in place. The elder selection policy spelled out, step-by-step, the entire process of selecting a new elder. The elder selection policy became a reference point in the constitution that would allow us to have the framework of the elements involved in selecting new elders. The policy was simply a detailed guideline for us to follow until we could implement the constitutional changes that were necessary.

The Wording of the Constitution. The original wording of the constitution had nothing in it that mandated the particular structure we have outlined here. Therefore, we felt it was necessary to add into the constitution wording that would guarantee that a prospective elder had to go through the process outlined in this book.

The new wording of the constitution in the election of the elders was changed to the following (bolded was the new addition):

"The elders shall be elected from the active membership at the annual election, **based upon three evaluations which include: a personal evaluation, an elder evaluation, and a congregational evaluation according to the church policy on the selection of elders,** for a term of three years with terms so arranged that the majority will not go out of office at the same time. After serving their term of office, elders cannot be re-elected as an elder or elected as a deacon until one year has passed."

Once the new process was in place and the first prospective elder was voted in, we changed the following items as well. We changed the constitution to remove the term-limit that had been in place. We kept a definite term that an elder would serve, which was three years, but we allowed them to serve consecutive terms. We did this to help men realize they did not have to serve indefinitely, and we did this to help the congregation realize they would have a chance to play an active role in encouraging and helping a man who may need to take a break from being an elder. We also changed the election percentage requirement to match that of the pastor. Now a prospective elder must get at least a seventy-five percent vote by the congregation, affirming him as an elder. The new constitutional wording has now been changed to:

"The elders, with the exception of the pastoral staff, shall be elected from the active membership; based upon three evaluations, which include: a personal evaluation, an elder evaluation, and a congregational evaluation according to the church policy on the selection of elders; for a term of three years and will be able, based upon a confirming vote of the congregation between terms at a properly called business meeting, to serve consecutive terms of three years. All elders must receive a 75% vote of confirmation from the congregation."

The reason that the election percentage and term limits were changed after the first prospective elder had come forward, is that we needed to make sure that the new process had been implemented and approved before we made the term limit change. In the process of making the term limit change, we realized that we needed to change the voting percentage to coincide with the plurality of eldership that we had supposedly believed in all along, but had failed to actually practice. By the time we could work our way through these particular changes, we had already brought along the prospective elder and had voted him in. The new changes applied to any man who had gone through the selection process.

Implementing the elder selection process had its challenges. We attempted to not just force something on the people, but rather we wanted to take the time to methodically teach, train, instruct, allow time for processing and allow an opportunity to ask questions as we went along. We didn't do everything perfectly I am sure, but I believe that by God's grace, we witnessed His sovereign hand in the entire process as He guided us to move through the elder selection process and its implementation.

What to do if your church has a nominating committee?

Many churches use a nominating committee for their selection process. In his commentary on Acts, Crawford offers that the "simplest" way to select elders is through a nominating committee."[37] There are various guiding philosophies for this

---

[37] C. C. Crawford, *Sermon Outlines on Acts* (Cincinnati, OH: Standard, 1919), 222–223. Crawford's suggestion is as follows: A day should be set aside, usually the first Lord's Day of the year, to attend to this business. Have three services on this day. Elect the officers at the morning hour, ordain them in the proper way at the afternoon service, and conduct the evening evangelistic service in the usual manner. The entire day should be given to prayer, fasting and ordination. Let this day be thoroughly advertised, so that every member will be present. Nothing should be done in a corner, or by a

practice. For instance, as McMullin shares in light of rural churches, "Holding an office in many rural churches has little to do with function. Often there is no nominating committee; many officers simply serve perpetual terms."[38] Others view the nominating committee as sort of a filter for the rest of their church. "The nominating committee may be the most important committee in our church, because it serves like the headwaters of a river. If there's pollution upstream, it will eventually defile everything downstream."[39] Others still go further to recognize the shortcomings of a nominating committee. "In the traditional system, a nominating committee would have put Saul, the tentmaker from Tarsus, on the maintenance committee. Men like Saul will cheerfully do this work, but they need a way to discover other gifts."[40]

In the case where a church decides to use a nominating committee for the various functional roles of the church, it is still good to provide oversight and leadership for the committee. It is dangerous for a church to relegate full authority and power to a nominating committee. There should be partnership. The elders should always be seen as the final oversight of all matters of a

---

faction, or in the spirit of partisanship. When the nominations are made by the committee at the morning service, let the final vote be taken by ballot, in case there might be danger of any dissension. Let everything be done decently and in order.

[38]Stephen McMullin, "How to Understand the Rural Mind-Set," in *Growing Your Church through Evangelism and Outreach*, ed. Marshall Shelley, 1st ed., Library of Christian Leadership (Nashville, TN: Moorings, 1996), 98.

[39]Larry W. Osborne, *The Unity Factor: Getting Your Church Leaders Working Together*, vol. 20, The Leadership Library (Carol Stream, IL: Christianity Today, Inc., 1989), 43. Osborne goes on to mention that his church uses the elders in this capacity: "In our case, our elder board serves as the final nominating committee. While there are obviously some potential problems with a standing board functioning as its own nominating committee, these are the best people we've got, so we use them." p. 45. I like that Osborne seems to have found a blended balance between elders and their functioning much like a nominating committee.

[40]Roberta Hestenes, "Turning Committees into Community," in *Growing Your Church through Training and Motivation: 30 Strategies to Transform Your Ministry*, ed. Marshall Shelley, vol. 4, Library of Leadership Development (Minneapolis, MN: Bethany House, 1997), 139.

church. However, for selecting a treasurer, clerk, nursery coordinator, or any other office a church may have, a nominating committee is a great tool.

The natural question out of this entire section may just be, "so what?" What difference does it make if a church uses a nominating committee to select their elders? The issue is not with nominating committees in general. If your church needs to elect a treasurer, or a clerk, or some other officer other than deacon or elder, then a nominating committee fits perfectly for that. Those positions in a church, are not addressed in Scripture. However, since Scripture does present to us a series of markers that must be present when choosing leadership, it is the obligation of churches to follow the prescribed markers of Scripture.

Churches who utilize a nominating committee to select leadership (elders/deacons) are not allowing Scripture to guide them and be their authority for faith and practice. The argument that a nominating committee is necessary in this process of selecting elders and deacons is as fallacious as the argument that states that a church must have Sunday School or a Sunday evening service in order to be a biblical church. What did churches do before Mr. Robert came along with the instructions on nominating committees and their role in selecting officers?

The problem with many evangelical churches in America today is that they have allowed themselves to no longer do the work that Scripture calls them to do. To put it in more abrupt terms, they have become lazy. It appears, as Merkle points out, that many churches "gave up and opted for a more conventional (though less biblical) model."[41] They would rather have a group of people select their leaders for them, than to do the often times difficult chore of

---

[41]Benjamin Merkle, *Why Elders?* (Grand Rapids: Kregel, 2009), 63. Merkle states that many churches have become so "professional" that "many congregations will not even consider hiring a person as their pastor unless he has a 'Dr.' in front of his name."

examining the men in their church who could serve in leadership. They are content to blame things on a committee for not nominating a person. instead of looking out over the congregants that God has sovereignly brought to that assembly and find the men who God may want to serve in the position of leadership. Furthermore, they should be identifying men who could potentially move into that role.

If we believe, and we should, that God is sovereign, then we have to not only believe that He is sovereign in the selection process but we must also put that belief into practice by following, as close as possible, to the process laid out for us in Scripture. To not do this, is to commit an "act of suicide." The reason many churches in America are not functioning as they should is because at some point, they allowed pragmatism to replace authoritative Scripture. It is time for churches everywhere to have the intestinal fortitude and love for Christ to do the right thing when it comes to selecting the elders who will serve in their churches.

What to do during a transition period?

On the back of the shampoo bottle is the phrase: wash, rinse, repeat. The best thing to remember during a time of transition is teach, model, repeat. It cannot be overemphasized enough the importance of this principle. Whether you are transitioning to elders or you are transitioning to a new selection process, the congregation is going to need to be taught the truths of God's word on this matter. However, teaching alone is not sufficient. You must model the Biblical application of what you are teaching. So let's talk about that.

Teach

George Bernard Shaw stated that, "The single biggest problem in communication is the illusion that it has taken place." From experience, I can say that this is certainly a true statement. Nothing seems more frustrating than when you feel as though you have communicated something fairly well and fairly often only to find that the audience to whom you are speaking seems to not get what was being communicated. I can remember one particular case in point where I had just finished a 6-week series on elders and then a 3-week series on deacons. I had passionately argued for the clear distinction between the two roles, and I felt that it was pretty clear that they had completely separate functions in the church. I felt like we had communicated pretty clearly on the matter. As I walked out to the lobby after the final service, an older man approached me and said, "I am not sure why this is such a big deal that you spent these past several weeks talking about this. Call them elders, call them deacons, call them trustees, they all do the same thing!" Needless to say, I was crushed that obviously we had the illusion that communication had taken place but clearly, it had not.

Even though you may feel as though you have communicated and even though people "nod their head" seeming to acknowledge that they have heard you and even seem to be "tracking" with you, it is imperative to continually teach and re-teach and teach again. Whether you are transitioning to elders or you are implementing a new model of selecting elders or you are just wanting to give a "refresher" on elders, you will do well to teach often on the matter. This does not mean that you have to take several messages just on elders per se, but it does mean that as you have opportunity you take those opportunities to teach on the matter.

Model

It has been said that your talk talks and you walk talks, but your walk talks louder than your talk talks! Not only is that a mouthful to try to say, but it is a true statement in that people will place more stock in how you live than they will in what you say. So, for instance, when you talk about the plurality of elders, you must seek to model that as best as you can. Even when you are going through a time of transition, the current elders haven't gone through any kind of qualifying process, and they do not want to serve as elders but they have decided it is better to fill out their term than to resign, you must still seek to model the plurality concept as much as you possibly can.

I will say that modeling a proper biblical model of plurality is extremely difficult, especially when you are transitioning through a situation that is less than biblical. However, I believe that the rewards that you will reap from the congregation will pay off in a large way as you strive to model the biblical process. You will certainly not always understand and appreciate the hard-work that is necessary as you model biblical truths, but the congregation will see it and whether they fully realize it or not, they will respond positively to the supremacy of Scripture as it is played out in the body.

A transition team

One of the key components that we utilized was a transition team of ordained men who were able to help us as we transitioned from men who had not been through any type of qualification process to men who had been through a qualifying process. This was, I believe, an important part of the transition. We did not feel as though we could allow the men who had not been certified to put together a certifying plan. Therefore, we found men who had been ordained and had them help us in developing the elder selection process. This may mean having to go outside of your particular church to find men who would be willing to help you with this, but this will lend a great deal of credibility to the new process.

What about elder rule vs. elder led (How to engage the congregation)?

There are certainly a number of opinions and thoughts on the extent of the elder's involvement in the decision-making process for a church. Some churches will hold to an elder-rule model while others will hold to an elder-led model. Each model will determine a bit differently how the elder selection process is played out. As we examine each of these options below, the key to remember is that each position has merit within a biblical model of polity.

The elder-rule model would be best defined by the fact that the elders of the church will make all of the decisions for the church. The congregation will have little, if any, say in the various decisions of the church. This is not to say that the congregation does not have a voice or some sort of input in the decisions that are made. Some churches will use surveys or other forms of communication feedback to find out where the congregation is on a particular matter, but all in all, the elders are responsible for decisions.

The elder-led model would be best defined by the fact that the elders of the church will make most of the decisions, but on larger or more significant decisions, the congregation will be given a vote for input. The elders will typically communicate what they feel is the direction that God wants the church to go, but ultimately, they would hold that the congregation bears responsibility in the decision making process as well. Those who operate within the elder-led model would believe that there can exist a balanced harmony between the congregation and the elders in the decision making process.

So, let's say that you are part of an elder-rule church. The challenge that will exist in this model is how do you as elders, who are making the decisions regarding prospective elders, account for the entire character of the prospective elder? In other words, how do you find out how this prospective elder behaves outside the church when the church is not gathering? Below are three suggestions on how you can best engage in this process.

Shepherding – One way that you as current elders can find out how the prospective elder is in his character and in his family is through intense shepherding. In other words, you spend the time necessary engaged in this man's life in order to know as much about him as you personally can. You see the responsibility as falling directly on you and you see your assessment as primary in the selection process. Part of this shepherding will include how he interacts with other congregants of the church. You may not be directly engaging the body in the process as much as you are watching how he conducts himself and interacts in the relationship with other believers.

Survey – Another way that you as the current elders can find out about the prospective candidate is to send out surveys to the congregation and get their candid feedback on his character. From his integrity to his self control to his children and his family life, you should be seeking to get as candid of responses as possible to determine what kind of character this man has. Again, because you are elder-rule, you as the elders will be making the ultimate decision about this man, but for your own ability to make a decision regarding this man, you will seek the feedback of those who most likely know him better in certain contexts than you do.

Panel – One other way for you to engage the congregation in the process of selecting elders is to utilize the panel format. This is not as popular a process, but it does give you access to a small sampling of congregants. How you intentionally structure this particular panel is really up to you. You may want to get a sampling of congregants that have regular interaction and engagement with the prospective elder. Again, you aren't soliciting the entire congregation, but you are being proactive in how you gain information that will be helpful to you in making the decision on whether or not this man is an elder.

So let's say that you are an elder-led church. The challenge that will exist in this process is how to make sure that you have engaged congregants who see the weight and importance of the elder selection process. Again, you believe that the congregation should be involved in the selection process, so as you scan the congregation you realize that some of them are not as spiritually mature as you would like. So, how do you make sure that those who will be voting on this man to be elder are serious about the process? Below are three suggestions on how to ensure the commitment of the congregation in this process.

Discipleship – Spending one on one time is an invaluable tool for you as the pastor or as leadership to be able to talk with and talk through any possible misunderstandings that a congregant may have. I have found this to be one of the best ways to be able to go deeper with someone and be able to probe to see where they may not be clear on a matter or where they may be thinking in a way that is not biblically accurate. This is also a great way to challenge those who are spiritually immature with Scripture to help guide them in a proper understanding of what God's word has to say.

Patience – Another way of helping the congregation through the process of being ready to select an elder is to demonstrate patience with the congregation. It is a temptation to try to expedite the process of bringing a man on as elder simply for pragmatics or for necessity. However, you are doing yourself, this man, and the congregation a disservice when you attempt to rush the process. Giving the congregation time to process this model and giving them time to think it through and come up with questions that you can answer as well as for them to just be able to take time to search Scripture will be the biggest blessing you can give. Allow the Spirit to work in the hearts of your congregation and allow them the time they need to be ready to select elders.

Interaction – A third thing that you can do as leadership that ultimately combines parts of the other two aspects is to provide as much interaction between the prospective candidate and the congregation as possible. This will accomplish several things. It will allow the prospective elder to be able to spend time engaging and discipling parts of the congregation. It will allow the congregation to engage and spend time with the prospective elder. The more interaction you can facilitate between the congregation and prospective candidates the more likely you are to see the congregation not only take the process seriously, but also, see them form invaluable relationships with the prospective candidate.

These may not be all of the questions you have as you go through this process, but these are some of the elements of implementing the elder selection process that we encountered. The greatest advice I can give is seek wisdom from God, seek wisdom from others who have gone through this, and seek wisdom from within the body. Be willing to be vulnerable to admit you do not have all the answers. Be willing to be humble and learn and grow and admit your mistakes along the way. The congregation will gravitate to that type of transparency.

10

Letting You See Our Cards......

Right or wrong, this is how we did it

The following is the overview of the different questions we asked for the different categories of information we were seeking from the prospective candidate for elder. We compiled all of his answers including the answers to his doctrinal follow-up questions that we had, and put this in a packet that we gave out to the congregation of our church before we did the congregational review. This will give you a brief glimpse into the whole process as we handled it. This is not intended to be something that you have to copy or try to duplicate, rather, this is simply our way of showing our process and how we allowed the selection process to play out.

Personal Evaluation and Assessment for Prospective Elders

1. Based on I Timothy 3:1 that the word "desire" is synonymous with the "call" of the elder, how have you seen the "desire" to be an elder confirmed in your life?

2. State Yes or No to this question: Given that we are all sinners saved by grace, and based upon Paul's writing in I Timothy 3, do you believe that you are growing in Christ-likeness and that by His grace you are qualified to be an elder?

3.   If you are not elected to be an elder, what will your response be?

4.   Why do you want to be an elder at WBC?

5.   Have you fulfilled the role of Shepherding at WBC? If so, how have you done that?

6.   What is your vision for WBC and the community it serves?

7.   Is your wife and/or children in favor of you serving as an elder at WBC?

8.   Are you willing to put in the amount of time that will be expected of a lay elder (avg.10-15 hrs./month)?

9.   Please provide us with the names and contact information for at least 3 personal references. This can be a friend, co-worker, or neighbor. Please indicate whether these people are believers. Please include at least two contacts who are not believers.

Doctrinal Interview Questions for Prospective Elder

The Gospel

- Please share your personal testimony

- What is the message of the gospel?

- How is this message lived out?

- What assurance do you have of eternal life?

- Have you been baptized by immersion after salvation? Why or why not?

The Church

- Describe the biblical model of government for the church

- What are the major priorities and duties of an elder?

- What are the roles of men/women in the church?

- Is church membership important? Why or why not?

- Describe how to handle the discipline of a sinning member?

- Describe the work of the Holy Spirit in the believer's life as church members

Lifestyle

- What is your philosophy on the elder's use of alcohol?

- What are your personal spiritual disciplines?

- What is your position on marriage and divorce?

- Describe your biblical role as a Father and Husband

General Doctrinal Questions

- Describe the person and work of Christ

- Describe the Trinity

- What is your position on creation?

- Describe the spiritual warfare believers are engaged in

- What are the sign gifts and are they applicable today?

- What is your position on Israel and the Church (covenant vs. dispensational)?

- What is your view of salvation in terms of God's sovereignty and man's responsibility?

- Which current authors or church history figures have most influenced your theology?

Please share with us in 1-2 pages how you intend to shepherd the flock at our church?

Questions for Personal References

Reference from Saved Boss for Prospective Elder

1. How would you describe the candidate's integrity in how he handles the matters revolving around his job requirements?

2. How would you describe his interaction with his co-workers? Does he behave differently with those who are believers as opposed to those who are not believers?

3. How would you describe his overall "attitude of life"? Does he complain, does he exhibit joyfulness, is he a pleasant person to be around?

Reference from Unsaved Neighbor for Prospective Elder

1. Tell me about his character as a neighbor

2. Tell me about how his family functions

3. Tell me about his willingness to help you out

4. Tell me about how he has tried to build a relationship with you

Reference for candidate from saved, former co-worker

1. How would you describe the candidate's desire to minister to other people?

2. How would you describe his desire to build relationships with unsaved people?

3. How would you describe the candidate's desire to glorify God in all he does?

Reference for candidate from unsaved man who works near candidate.

1. From what you know of the candidate, what would you say has made the biggest impression on you as far as how he conducts himself in the workplace?

2. From what you know of Him, would you say that he is a man who can be trusted and depended upon?

3. From what you know about him, would you say that what he says he believes and practices as a Christian is consistent with how he lives his life?

We mentioned elsewhere that this process took us about a year to complete with each candidate. This is a good length of time to take to go through this. This give everyone involved time to pray, study, respond, and answer with wisdom and confidence. When we put the packet together with all of this information to the congregation, we gave it to them six to eight weeks before we had the candidate interview with the congregation. This gave the congregation ample time to read and review the candidates answers and be able to personally engage with the candidate. The key to this is do not rush this process! Take your time and allow God to work to seamlessly bring everyone together as only He can!

Conclusion

"To compromise on leadership is the most suicidal act a church can commit." Spurgeon was certainly right in his assessment of the implications of a church having bad leadership. You don't have to wait long to hear about various churches across the country that have had to remove their lead pastor or other elders because of sin. Nor do you have to look far to see churches that are simply functioning with severe anemia. Satan has done a masterful job of causing strife, divisions, and discontent within the body. Churches who are devoid of biblical leadership are especially susceptible to attacks and are easily destroyed by Satan. We know that ultimately, the universal church of Christ will not be destroyed. We know that the gates of hell will not persevere against it. However, this is no guarantee that a specific local assembly is not immune from Satan's attacks and that the possibility that the local church could be destroyed is a real danger.

This book has attempted to take you through a logical and methodical basis for and process for selecting elders in your church. Again, I know that many of you will be in various places in this entire process and that a one size fits all model is not necessarily a good thing. However, I do hope that I have been able to convincingly show you the need for your church having a biblical process in place for selecting lay elders. Without the biblical model in place, a church is leaving themselves wide open for attacks, divisions, confusion, and outright sin in how they handle the selection of their elders.

Too many churches have looked at the daunting nature of an overhaul or implementation of this model and have decided to let pragmatism take control and simply not do anything about the current model that is in their church. Implementing this process is daunting, time consuming and at times difficult, but I can assure you from experience that you will not regret doing the hard things and help your church to implement an elder selection process in your church. Believers have an amazing resource in the Holy Spirit who is capable of giving us the strength and giving the congregation the grace and ability to work through the process to change or implement the elder selection process.

Again, we know that this is not the only way that a lay elder can and should be selected, but hopefully it is a model that is not just biblical, but is also practical. We hope that you will prayerfully consider what has been written in this book and use the principles here for the honor and glory of God in your church as you seek to select the men that God has called and equipped to be the shepherds of His flock. We desire that all praise and glory go to God for any help that this has been. May God bless you as you seek to honor and glorify Him in the matter of selecting shepherds who will image the Chief Shepherd to the local congregation.

Thank you for the opportunity to help you think through some of these things! God is more than faithful and I am confident that He will be more than faithful to you in this process. May God bless you and your congregation as you seek to be faithful to His word in implementing a process like this and may you see His blessing on you as you continue to follow Him in your church.

Made in the
USA
Monee, IL